The Samuel & Althea Stroum Lectures
in Jewish Studies

The Samuel & Althea Stroum Lectures
in Jewish Studies

Imagining
Russian Jewry

~

Memory

History

Identity

Steven J. Zipperstein

UNIVERSITY OF WASHINGTON PRESS

Seattle & London

Library of Congress Cataloging-in-Publication Data

Zipperstein, Steven J., 1950–
Imagining Russian Jewry : memory, history, identity /
Steven J. Zipperstein.
p.   cm. — (The Samuel & Althea Stroum lectures in Jewish studies)
Includes bibliographical references and index.
ISBN 0-295-97789-2 (cloth : alk. paper). —
ISBN 0-295-97790-6 (paper : alk. paper)
1. Jews—Russia—Historiography.   2. Memory.   3. Jews—Russia—
Public opinion.   4. Public opinion—Jews.   5. Public opinion—
United States.   6. Jews—Russia—Intellectual life.   7. Jews—
Ukraine—Odessa—Historiography.   8. Holocaust, Jewish
(1939–1945)—Europe, Eastern—Historiography.   I. Title.
II. Series: Samuel and Althea Stroum lectures in Jewish studies.
DS135.R9Z67   1999
947′.004924—dc21   98-53887
CIP

The Samuel & Althea Stroum Lectures
in Jewish Studies

Samuel Stroum, businessman, community leader, and philanthropist, by a major gift to the Jewish Federation of Greater Seattle, established the Samuel and Althea Stroum Philanthropic Fund.

In recognition of Mr. and Mrs. Stroum's deep interest in Jewish history and culture, the Board of Directors of the Jewish Federation of Greater Seattle, in cooperation with the Jewish Studies Program of the Henry M. Jackson School of International Studies at the University of Washington, established an annual lectureship at the University of Washington known as the Samuel and Althea Stroum Lectureship in Jewish Studies. This lectureship makes it possible to bring to the area outstanding scholars and interpreters of Jewish thought, thus promoting a deeper understanding of Jewish history, religion, and culture. Such understanding can lead to an enhanced appreciation of the Jewish contributions to the historical and cultural traditions that have shaped the American nation.

The terms of the gift also provide for the publication from time to time of the lectures or other appropriate materials resulting from or related to the lectures.

To my parents,

Mae and Edward Zipperstein

He shall turn the hearts of fathers toward their children and
the hearts of children toward their fathers.

—Malachi 3:26

Our literary and cultural history is full of the records of romances with other cultures or, sometimes, with other classes. Haunted as we all are by unquiet dreams of peace and wholeness, we are eager and quick to find them embodied in another people. Other peoples may have for us the same beautiful integrity that, from childhood on, we are taught to find in some period of our national or ethnic past. Truth, we feel, must somewhere be embodied in man. Ever since the nineteenth century, we have been fixing on one kind of person or another, to satisfy our yearning. . . . everyone searching for innocence, for simplicity, and integrity of life.

—Lionel Trilling, "The Situation of the
American Intellectual at the Present Time"

~

We could put it quite simply. Gemeinschaft is the paradise of memory. But as Proust asserted in a celebrated aphorism, the only paradises we have are the ones we have lost. Their distance from our present is always infinite.

—Richard Terdiman, *Present Past:*
Modernity and the Memory Crisis

Contents

Acknowledgments

This book, brief as it may be, owes a great deal to many friends, colleagues, and several generous institutions. First, I thank the faculty in the Jewish Studies Program at the University of Washington, Seattle, for hosting me with such flair and warmth in May 1995 at the Samuel and Althea Stroum Lectures. I recall that ten-day period with fondness. I thank Hillel Kieval, Martin Jaffe, Robert Stacey, as well as Dorothy Becker, the program administrator at the time. I am grateful to the Stroums, of course, for their continued support of Jewish scholarship.

I did much of the reading for this book as a Fellow at the Institute for Advanced Studies at the Hebrew University in Jerusalem in 1993–94. I thank the organizers of that yearlong research seminar on East European Jewish history, the Fellows, and staff at the Institute for helping to make this time so productive and stimulating. In 1998, while a Fellow at the Stanford Humanities Center, and at work on another book, I put the final touches on this manuscript. My research has been supported at Stanford by the Daniel E. Koshland Fund for Jewish Culture and History and by the Taube Faculty Research Fund of the Program in Jewish Studies.

I thank the librarians at Stanford's Green Library for their skill and patience, especially Roger Kohn, who, until recently, was its Curator of Judaica. I also thank Sonia Moss, head of Stanford's interlibrary loan office. I remain grateful, as always,

Acknowledgments

to Zachary Baker, Librarian of the YIVO Institute for Jewish Research. I received assistance from the staffs at the archive and library at the Jewish National and University Library at the Givat Ram campus of the Hebrew University, Jerusalem, and at GARF, the State Archives of the Russian Federation, in Moscow.

Daily conversations with my Stanford colleague Aron Rodrigue enriched this manuscript, and I thank him for his wisdom and friendship. I owe much to Keith Baker, Arnold Eisen, Norman Naimark, Amir Weiner, and Talya Fishman (who, as a Visiting Professor at Stanford from Rice University, read a draft with unusual care). Friends outside Stanford— Tony Judt and Eli Lederhendler—also read the manuscript at various stages and offered suggestions and criticisms. Mitchell Cohen helped sharpen the book, as did my Russian history teacher, Hans Rogger, who provided characteristically meticulous, wise counsel. I am also grateful to my research assistant, Abraham Socher.

I discussed aspects of the book with my Ph.D. students in Jewish history, whose reactions helped a great deal. Mitchell Hart, a former Ph.D. student of mine and now Assistant Professor at Florida International University, offered insightful suggestions. Among my last conversations with my late Jewish history teacher, Amos Funkenstein, was a talk about this work, and I recall this, and my other exchanges with this remarkable scholar, with gratitude.

I thank my editors, Naomi Pascal and Pamela Bruton, at the University of Washington Press for their high standards and their gentle prodding. I'm grateful for the help of the splendid staff in the Program in Jewish Studies at Stanford, Julia Erwin Weiner and Susan Harwood, and Sean Forner in Stanford's Department of History.

I learned much from the responses of colleagues and

Acknowledgments

others at the various universities where I delivered versions of these chapters. In particular, I am grateful to Professor Nancy Green and the participants in the fall 1997 seminars I delivered as a Visiting Professor at the École des Hautes Études en Sciences Sociales. Papers drawn from this book were also given at the Stanford Humanities Center; the UCLA Center for European Studies; the University of Michigan, Ann Arbor; Jagiellonian University; the Institute for Advanced Studies, Hebrew University, Jerusalem; and the National Yiddish Book Center, at Hampshire College. Chapter 3 of this book was published, in somewhat different form, in *Jewish Social Studies: History, Culture, and Society* 2, no. 2 (winter 1996).

My wife, Sally Goodis, appears, in one way or another, on every page of this book, much as she has in everything I've done since we met more than twenty years ago. Whatever I may have come to learn about life, and joy, outside the study, I owe her. My sons, Max and Sam, now aged eleven and nine, are both, at times, bemused by what it is I do as a historian; perhaps this book, once they read it, will answer one or another of their questions. Beginning, and ending, nearly every day together with them remains an incalculable pleasure. I thank my parents for all that a son brings from childhood. I dedicate this book to them, with love.

Stanford, California
July 1998

Imagining Russian Jewry

Memory, History, Identity

Prologue

"A historiographical anxiety arises when history assigns itself the task of tracing alien impulses within itself and discovers that it is the victim of memories which it has sought to master."[1] So writes French historian Pierre Nora. This book examines such a moment. It looks at the relationship between history and metaphor in the ways in which the Russian Jewish past has been understood in the last century. I examine this theme in the form of essays that reflect on how to think about a complex milieu with its surplus of memory, its horrors, and its splendid intellectual surprises.[2]

The topics discussed in this book tend to fall just beyond the pages of most formal discussions of Jewish history. Popular memory of the past has, when noted by Jewish historians, been disparaged as a source of knowledge, and it is nearly always as factual errors that such memories are mentioned, if at all, in works of historical scholarship. I seek in these essays to challenge some of the barriers between professional and popular knowledge of this world. What interests me is how in the last century the past has been remembered and forgotten, how it has been integrated and unsettled in popular, as well as professional, accounts, and what the intrusion of memory has meant for the writing of history itself. What interests me is the interrelationship between various ways of understanding the past. This, then,

3

Prologue

is a book about books, a reflection on reading, collective memory, history, and the often uneasy—and also uncomfortably intimate—relationships that exist between seemingly incompatible ways of seeing the past.

This surplus of memory that I describe with regard to Russian Jewry—the spawning ground of much of the mass migration in the first decades of this century—is amply illustrated by the range of salient images in contemporary Jewish life inspired by it: pogroms, shtetl, and (rather more distantly) kibbutz. Immigrant memory in the United States, and elsewhere, too, tended to see this world almost entirely in dark terms. Such images were by no means displaced by the discovery (especially by American Jews beginning in the 1950s and 1960s) of the shtetl as an emblem of unencumbered identity and family peacefulness, a place where Jewish life was (or, so it was claimed) experienced as vividly as anywhere else in modernity.

To the extent to which ideology has had an impact on Jewish popular attitudes toward this past, above all, it is in terms of Zionism—the only Jewish political ideology to arise in Eastern Europe that survived into the mid–twentieth century. This movement was inspired, especially in its early years before the fall of the Russian empire, by a (mostly grim) sense of the lives of Jews under the tsars. Zionism's attitudes toward exile and relations between Gentiles and Jews solidified a coherent, bleak portrait of Jewish life in Russia. In the last half century, the Holocaust, the creation of the Israeli state, the obliteration of Jewish life in much of Eastern Europe, and its officially sanctioned dilution in Soviet Russia have similarly lent a heightened authority to such readings.

Still more influential, however, were more recent inspirations of other sorts. In the last half century, Russia has come to be seen in America as the focus of pedigree, as an object of

4

Prologue

nostalgia. In the popular Jewish imagination this past has come to represent, in various ways, a self-reflexive yardstick for the successes and failures of contemporary Jewish life as imagined against the backdrop of a world fixed in time in a rarefied, obliterated place.[3] This, to be sure, constitutes a shift, for before the 1950s American Jews typically remembered Russia mostly for its brutish, unpredictable violence. Later, too, pogroms would continue to serve as an influential metaphor for Russian Jewish life, but the region would also now remind Jews of good as well as bad things: of the comfortable, reassuring joys of family, piety, community, spirituality, of a suppposedly seamless, holistic way of life left behind in the rush for the bounty of social mobility.

Russia, the locus of pogroms, was now also the site of the shtetl. Few terms evoke quite so vividly for Jews the wages of modernity, what was abandoned to achieve what they now have. American literary critic Alfred Kazin wrote in 1966: "Jews don't believe in original sin. They certainly believe in the original love that they once knew in the shtetl, in the kitchen, in the Jewish household."[4]

The relationship between these impulses and the writing of history is at the center of this book. Popular assumptions about this region have left an imprint on our work, as historians, that is too significant to be relegated to the margins. By no means, of course, have Jewish historians been unaware of the many, often fiercely argued assumptions about the world we write about. But their intrusion into our historical work has been carefully monitored based on the assumption that what we, as historians, do must remain unaffected by the ferocity of folk memory, for stark, definitive barriers exist between these irrevocably different, even oppositional routes to viewing the past. Indeed, divisions between popular and scholarly assumptions have been more vigorously

Prologue

maintained in the writing of the history of East European Jewish life than perhaps in writing on any other aspect of modern Jewish history.

The (reputedly) dispassionate texture of East European Jewish historical writing is a stark, if understandable reaction to a shrillness that we know all too well. Most of us who write this history have lived in close proximity to survivors of this world, with their stories, their often repetitive tales, at times noble, at times exasperating. We've heard them describe this world as relentlessly dark and dreadful; we've also heard of it as a splendid, holistic community where, before it was leveled, Jews were happily free to be themselves. When, later, we produced our own historical work, such voices were (or so we told ourselves) hushed, their all-too-often ahistorical, decontextualized narratives unsettled, or at least challenged, by what we wrote. And, indeed, they were. Still, the empiricism of our scholarship was, in turn, exaggerated in an effort to establish the clearest boundaries between (the imperfections of) memory and (the solidity of) history.

Unlike the historians of Sicilian or Irish immigrants to America, historians of East European Jewry know that the very ground we study is, by and large, a graveyard of Jewish life, all the more eerily evocative and awful to encounter because of what is no longer there. To write about this world as if we are not aware of this fate (as a good many historians of East European Jewry, myself included, have in the recent past sought to do) is, I'm now convinced, unrealistic, an antiseptic enterprise that overlooks the moral underpinnings and humanity implicit in any historical enterprise. This book seeks to reexamine the interaction between these seemingly contradictory ways of understanding the past.

My use of the terms "collective memory" or "folk memory" is inspired by sociologist Maurice Halbwachs, whose

Prologue

influential work examined how constructions of the past in collective memory have served to sustain collective life in the present. In such exercises, he insisted, it is the present that looms largest in attempts to project "our concepts on the conditions of the past." Halbwachs's distinction between historicism and collective memory is useful, but as my late teacher Amos Funkenstein argued, they are too stark: even collective memory remains informed by (what Funkenstein calls) historical consciousness. Moreover, as Funkenstein writes, "thinking about history reflected the moods and sentiments of the community in which this thinking took place."[5] Responding to Yosef Hayim Yerushalmi's important study *Zakhor: Jewish History and Jewish Memory*, he argues that because of his indebtedness to Halbwachs, Yerushalmi deemphasized the interplay between collective memory and historical consciousness in representations of the Jewish past. According to Funkenstein, even liturgical exposition, which Yerushalmi saw as essentially free from historical awareness, embodied a major theme of historical reasoning: "an incessant astonishment at one's own existence."[6] Funkenstein locates the emergence of the first, coherent stages in Jewish historical consciousness in early-nineteenth-century Western and Central Europe as embodied in the Wissenschaft des Judentums, the albeit deeply engaged movement for a scholarly, scientific study of Judaism: "The collective memory of the community in which the Wissenschaft des Judentums was embedded shows a high degree of consonance in its fears and aspirations. Even if we grant that the majority of traditional Jews in France, Austria, and Germany were not aware of the full scope of the achievements of the Wissenschaft, its results nevertheless faithfully reflected their desires and the self-image of nineteenth-century Jews craving for emancipation, the mood of the 'perplexed of the times.'"[7]

Prologue

I find Funkenstein's argument persuasive, and consistent with it, I analyze here the relationship between various, often influential popular narratives of the Russian Jewish past— some of which, as I argue in the first chapter, find their way into American Jewish literature and, in turn, into the writing of history. This book evaluates the interplay between memory and history and, in the process, examines the pleasures and exasperations of writing critically and with empathy about one's own people's past.

Eudora Welty, a writer of fiction and essays from the American South who was much preoccupied with the place of ancestral space in one's work (and who had a devoted following among the producers of American Jewish fiction in the 1950s and 1960s), once observed: "writers must always write best of what they know, and sometimes they do it by staying where they know it. But not for safety's sake. Although it is in the words of a witch— or all the more because of that—a comment of Hecate's in *Macbeth* is worth our heed: 'Security / Is mortal's chiefest enemy.' In fact, when we think in terms of the spirit, which are the terms of writing, is there a conception more stupefying than that of security? Yet writing what you know has nothing to do with security: what is more dangerous?"[8]

The essays in this book are rather general in scope. They are intended to be suggestive, not definitive. All the chapters were originally lectures: three were delivered, in the spring of 1995, as Samuel and Althea Stroum Lectures in Jewish Studies at the University of Washington at Seattle; the fourth, I gave in winter 1997 as the keynote address for a UCLA Center for European Studies conference "Jewish Communities in Eastern Europe since the Holocaust." I wrote it, too, with the intention of including it in this book. I have not substantially altered the text of the original, spoken versions, so that they

Prologue

might retain their personal voice, their engagement, and also their sense of urgency.

The tone of these essays reflects my preoccupation with a range of often all-too-readily overlooked connections linking what historians do with the world beyond their desks. In this regard, I probe the relationship between images of an often reified, sanctified Russian Jewish past and their impact on contemporary Jewish identities, especially in the United States. This exercise is not exclusively an academic one; to be more precise, this is an academic exercise that is far from seeing itself as distant or dispassionate. At its core is an effort to point in the direction of how to write about the past in ways that balance critical scrutiny, self-awareness, and engagement.

A technical point: I describe this community as "Russian Jewry" because the approximately five million Jews who lived in the Russian empire at the turn of the twentieth century constituted, by far, the world's largest concentration of East European Jews. Still, it should be noted that the political boundaries separating, say, Austro-Hungarian Lvov (Lviv) from Bessarabian Kishinev, in the Russian empire, did not, in themselves, render the cities fundamentally distinct. Nor should we forget that throughout the East European region, Jews overwhelmingly spoke a Jewish language, Yiddish, and lived in the midst of considerable cultural heterogeneity, often side by side with several different, sometimes mutually hostile, or at least distrustful, minorities. In the Russian empire itself, where the majority of Jews lived in the fifteen provinces known as the Pale of Settlement, most resided in places where Russians were not the dominant ethnic group but rather Ukrainians, Poles, or Belorussians, and where interaction between these groups was often uneasy, especially with the assertion of national awareness beginning late in

Prologue

the nineteenth century. These multilayered, complex inter-actions have inspired at least one prominent Jewish historian to ask recently whether it is historically reasonable even to speak in terms of Russian Jewish history.[9] For the sake of convenience, I use the word "Russia" as a geographical, not a cultural, designation, and I do so with an awareness that the region itself was immeasurably more diverse than the term itself might, perhaps, imply.

Chapter 1 examines literary and other popular responses in America to the Old World, beginning with turn-of-the-century immigrant novels and culminating in the 1960s with *Fiddler on the Roof.* This chapter traverses much space and time as it sets down broad paradigms for understanding some of the uses to which the Russian Jewish past has been put. In Chapter 2, I attempt to unsettle what, in retrospect, may be seen as an excessively fixed, coherent sense of pre-revolutionary Russian Jewish culture. I analyze a widespread unease among turn-of-the-century Russian Jews themselves regarding their culture's viability and future, looking mostly at rather obscure figures whose voices are recorded in the transcripts (which I located in archives in Moscow and Jeru-salem) of teachers meetings. I find them so preocccupied with merely sustaining a fractured Russian Jewish culture that they were willing to actively support an otherwise dis-paraged educational institution, the heder, in the hope that it would check further cultural erosion. Chapter 3 studies how over the course of the last century the Russian Jewish past has been written and rewritten with particular reference to the history of Odessa, the empire's second-largest Jewish community. In this context, I examine my own abiding in-terest in this city in a rather discrete amalgam of themes that represent a useful interpretive framework to understand Jew-ish modernity. The last chapter evaluates—and criticizes—

Prologue

efforts to excise the impact of the Holocaust from historical constructions of the East European Jewish past written since the Shoah.

There is much in this book about writing: its anxieties, its evasions, its pleasures. So much of what historians do relies on a repertoire of intuitive skills, narrative strategies, and commitments usually associated with the writing of fiction. The lines separating these forms of narration are often rather elusive, a fluidity much too rarely appreciated.

The chasm—and the interrelationship—between historical knowledge and widely disseminated, often strongly felt, popular assumptions about the world of Russian Jewry (its pogroms, its poverty, its piety, etc.) are the unifying threads running through what might seem rather disparate chapters. The arguments I make are bolstered by my reading of recent critical literature on the relationship between history and memory (by David Lowenthal, Saul Friedlander, Yosef Hayim Yerushalmi, Amos Funkenstein, and others), which, in turn, has confirmed my sense of the importance of rethinking the various methods used to inscribe the East European Jewish past.[10]

Among the many pleasures of delivering the Stroum Lectures is the way in which they provide a framework for sustained reflection rather than primarily empirical research. It is in this spirit that I begin with a brief excursus that seeks to clarify something of the personal urgency—and also the interplay between resonant, conflicting images about the Russian Jewish past—which inspire this book.

I don't recall the word "Russia" mentioned much as I was growing up. Later, when I began to study the Russian language in the early 1970s, I couldn't help but notice the consternation of some family members, and even neighbors: odd, off-balance remarks about Lee Harvey Oswald's penchant for Russian, an anxiety so off-kilter, so disproportionate that, clearly, more was at stake than was articulated. I sensed, even then, that lingering fears of McCarthyism—and, perhaps, still vaguer anxieties—lay behind the outbursts. What these might have been I couldn't say and, given my age, they didn't detain me.

Now, these responses seem far from frivolous. They provide me, I think, with a key to various things left unsaid, sentences unfinished, statements of such apparently grand incoherence that no one could credit them (or, so I once thought) with seriousness, shavings of the past too raw or perplexing for our second-generation American Jewish household to understand.

My grandfather's townlet (on my father's side), Lahishin, a *dorf* (village) is what he and other relatives called it, was destroyed, or so I was told. The information seemed incontrovertible. Everyone I knew from Lahishin agreed, and I knew a good many people since my grandparents were members of a formal, rather active association, a landsmanshaft of those born in or near Lahishin, based in Chicago with branches, like ours, in Los Angeles and elsewhere. Lahishin, they explained, the place adjacent to the marshlands near Pinsk that had brought them together, was obliterated shortly after my grandfather fled in 1919 or 1920. Surprisingly little more was said about it. The geography of the place was eventually rendered still more obscure for me when my grandfather, soon before his death in the mid-1950s, insisted that he was born in Poland, not Russia or the Soviet Union, as I was certain he had said before. Russia, that fiercely politicized place, was now moved somewhere beyond Lahishin, and the birthplace of my father's family was gone, leveled by pogromists, its Jews decimated and scattered.

Prologue

Imagine my surprise when later I glanced at a road map of Belarus and noticed Lahishin, just off a main strip of highway, a small place with little to distinguish itself apparently but far from annihilated. I mentioned this to an uncle who had been born there, who smiled as if he wasn't much surprised.

There was, indeed, much that he and the others found themselves obliged to forget: Chashke, for instance, a woman with a smooth, childlike face in a house far from our Jewish neighborhood, a place full of birds, fresh flowers, and plants growing inside, a Yiddish-accented bohemia—it was the first such place I'd ever seen. Chashke, a landsman, disappeared from our circle when she took a relative to a picnic in Griffith Park that turned out to be a Communist Party rally. Years later, I chanced upon another relative who told me that great-uncles of mine had performed on the Chicago Yiddish stage. I had never heard their names before. "Communists," I was told, laconically, when I mentioned the encounter. In short, Lahishin had its formal Russian borders redrawn, Chashke was summarily dropped, great-uncles (and, presumably, others too) were written off, my grandparents' birthplace itself was erased by an association launched, at least formally, to recall it.

A past flattened into something relentlessly grim or (incredible as the juxtaposition may seem) insipid and sweet. Recently, I read for the first time with real care the Yiddish poems and memoirs written by my aunt Tserile Teplinsky, who died ten years before I was born and in whose memory I was named Tsvi.[11] Here I found that her recollections of life in Lahishin (some of which I recalled from readings from her manuscripts at our family's landsmanshaft) were in stark contrast to the tone of the poetry. The memoirs are, on the whole, predictable declamations about small-town Jewish life. In contrast, her poems, found unpublished in her drawer

Prologue

after her death, were complex, impressive explorations of desire, with more than a hint of sexual longing, forbidden in her deeply conservative milieu. When I mentioned my impressions of the love poems to my father, her youngest brother, who still recites with gusto lines from Tsirele's evocations of shtetl life, his response was much like the reply to my discovery of Lahishin on the Belarus road map: a vague acknowledgment, an expression of unwavering confidence in the immutability of the past that new evidence was unlikely to sunder.

~ 1 ~

Shtetls There and Here

Imagining Russia in America

In Gemeinschaft with one's family, one lives from birth on,
bound to it weal and woe. One goes into Gesellschaft as one
goes into a foreign country.
—M. Ferdinand Tonnies, *Community and Society*

~

Near the opening of Isaac Rosenfeld's 1946 novel *Passage from Home*, a Jewish adolescent in Chicago takes us to his family's Passover seder. Bernard Miller, now fourteen, will spend the next few months measuring his estrangement from family (especially his father) and from Jewry. "I had suddenly shot up—that is, in my own estimation—and it seemed to me that I towered over life. Life meant the family."[1] Bernard's father is morose and self-lacerating ("a serious man, a failure," Lionel Trilling's characterization of the father of Isaac Babel),[2] an American Jew without a sense of intimacy with a Jewish past, without much success and still less joy in the present, with little to show for a lifetime in America except for his own indeterminacy. And then, there is Bernard's grandfather: expansive, untidy, idle (by American standards, at least), an extravagant, pious Russian Jew who "always wore carpet slippers in the house, as if to show how thoroughly at home he felt"—moments of carelessness, of comfort unknown to Bernard's father. "Grandfather was an improvident man who lived like a king."[3]

One of the guests at the seder, a tattooed Tennessee hillbilly relative-by-marriage, is inspired by the melodies and sings country tunes, clapping loudly, endearing himself to the grandfather while plunging Bernard's father into a brooding sense of displacement. He cannot appreciate melodies from the heartland of America because, Rosenfeld implies, he is so

Shtetls There and Here

distant from his own natural home. Yet the grandfather, a warmhearted Hasid whose tiny Chicago synagogue is described with sympathy in the novel (a book celebrated at the time by Irving Howe, Daniel Bell, Diana Trilling, and others as perhaps the outstanding portrait of Jewish childhood in the United States), can enjoy Americana precisely because he is so comfortable with his own people. "Jews in America have relatively little contact with country life, with small town folk and farmers. But through cultural retention," Rosenfeld explains elsewhere, "through a subliminal orientation to more primitive surroundings, they may still find in themselves access to rural life, understanding its character and traditions."[4]

Here we encounter the assertion—rather surprising, really, in view of what Eastern Europe and Russia meant for American Jews for much of the century (i.e., pogroms, obscurantism)—that such connections deepen one's humanity, even one's appreciation for the magic of the world. In the short story "The World of the Ceiling," Rosenfeld's protagonist goes to the roof of his parent's apartment building in order to evoke a world of intensity, a Russia of fierce dark women, conspirators, menacing Cossacks, and rare beauty. Eventually he grows up. "Little by little I lost this power. I grew up, married, raised children, ran after them wiping their noses, and thus sank deeper and deeper into reality and, as my father had predicted, into poverty. I haven't had much time to spend on the ceiling. When I step out of the house I see no more troikas, aristocrats and revolutionaries. The ugly, narrow, crowded street in which we live, full of smoke and noise, is an ugly, narrow, crowded street—goodbye Nevsky Prospekt."[5]

It is, as Werner Sollors tells us in the *Harvard Encyclopedia of American Ethnic Groups*, from the vantage point of the roof that the literature on American life written by Jews in the

17

first decades of the twentieth century often sees Eastern Europe: Abraham Cahan's *Yekl*, that stunning final scene in Israel Zangwill's *Melting Pot*, the roof scenes in Henry Roth's lyrical *Call It Sleep*, even the hardheaded, antimetaphysical socialist realist Michael Gold has his *Jews without Money* transcend the streets and commune on a rooftop.[6]

My interest here is in what American Jewish writers saw, or thought they saw, across the waters from their rooftops. My agenda in this chapter is counterchronological, prompted by a desire to better understand present-day attitudes in a historical inquiry of various, often conflicting notions of the past. I use the words "Russia" and "Eastern Europe" interchangeably—inaccurately, of course, on technical grounds, but in this, an essay on perceptions over a century or so, formal, geographical boundaries are only one of many features of Old World life rendered metaphorically.

I could investigate this past in various ways—perhaps like anthropologist Jack Kugelmass, who in a fascinating article looked at Sammy's Romanian Steak House, a pricey Lower East Side eatery where East European Jewish traditions are parodied (and also idealized) by customers who don't know these traditions: "Sammy's is a fabricated universe . . . and what it has to offer is a past that no one ever had but many people think is theirs." Kugelmass could just as well have chosen the now-annual "Matzoh Meal, MuShu, and Mistletoe" celebration held in a San Francisco Chinese restaurant on Christmas Eve, where comedians entertain with Jewish themes (a recent *New York Times* piece lists these as hypochondria, Hebrew school, and prune juice) on an evening that ends with what the *Times* calls "the anthem of late 20th-century American yuppie Jewry, not 'Hatikva' or the Internationale, but 'Sunrise, Sunset.'"[7]

The evidence I prefer instead is a more formal set of texts

Shtetls There and Here

(a canon of sorts) consisting mostly of fiction (a rather familiar list by Abraham Cahan, Anzia Yezierska, Philip Roth, and others) and plays, including, of course, *Fiddler on the Roof*, the sturdiest source of popular contemporary wisdom on East European Jewry. I rely primarily on literary sources published in the English language. I do so because of their resonance in American culture and their impact on American Jews across the generations. These texts provide insight into moments of Jewish life that fall between the cracks of the more standard historical narratives about American Jewry; they offer, I think, a useful perspective on otherwise private moments that may be, in fact, more normative than those that transpire in the American synagogue or a Jewish communal venue.

There is, to be sure, no attempt here to comprehensively survey American Jews' preoccupations with Eastern Europe. This would demand an investigation of many more texts, a full range of Yiddish, as well as Hebrew, writing, theater in English and Yiddish, popular fiction, radio plays, movies, and television.[8] A comprehensive examination of these issues would also require an investigation into the cultural politics of silence. By this I mean, for instance, the failure to acknowledge the East European backdrop to American Jewish life in the copious writings of Mordecai Kaplan, the leading American Jewish theologian—a backdrop which, as a Lithuanian rabbinic prodigy, he knew intimately but never spoke about directly in his major work. The closest he came was his often-stated call for an "organic community," which was, presumably, inspired by recollections of his past.[9]

In the years since the Second World War, the Russian Jewish past emerged as a source of pedigree, as proof that Jews had previously personified spirituality, wholeness, and communal cohesion, perhaps also scholarly distinction. Although a violent, unpredictable place, it was also the scene of a common childhood when faith was steady, families were whole, and God favored his people. The European catastrophe, the search for identity and place in postwar America, the geographical dispersion of a previously urban American Jewry in the 1950s and beyond—all these had their impact on perceptions of an East European Jewish past that is, as we speak about it in this chapter, an American, not a Russian, story. We will examine, then, those moments in American Jewish life when perceptions of the "world of our fathers" were fixed, when the features of contemporary Jewish nostalgia were first elucidated.

"We have to be Americans. We will be." This is from a 1916 editorial in the *Forverts*. "We will learn English. We will accommodate ourselves to the laws and organization of the country. We will interest ourselves in its politics. . . . We will accomplish in the New World a hundred times more than we could in the Old. But you will not be able to erase the old home from your heart. The heart will be drawn elsewhere. And in your solitude, images will rise up and stare in your faces with eternal sorrow."[10] In terms of public discourse at least, as Ewa Morawska has demonstrated,[11] Eastern Europe impinged on immigrant Jewish life considerably less than it did on non-Jewish Poles or Lithuanians in the United States: there are fewer articles in the Yiddish press on the Old Home (except when news of fresh pogroms reached the United States) and more frequent and more positive references to the United States. This different tenor of Americanization can, perhaps, be traced to the fact that Jewish immigrants, in contrast to Poles, Lithuanians, or other non-Jews from the same native milieu, were less likely to feel that they had a homeland to which to return.

Shtetls There and Here

Indeed, as Morawska writes in her analysis of turn-of-the-century newspaper coverage of Eastern Europe and Russia in the Polish- and Yiddish-language press in America: "In striking contrast to Slavic newspapers, preoccupied with their parts of Eastern Europe, the Jewish press gave relatively limited coverage to the topics of Russia and Austria-Hungary apart from reports on anti-Semitism. . . . For readers of Yiddish newspapers, Eastern Europe's connection with reports of hostile actions against Jews emphasized the . . . disassociation, or Jewish otherness from that larger society. The much more frequent, positive references to America as *undzer land* (Yiddish: our land) promoted positive associative images of the new environment."[12]

Still, as the *Forverts* editorial implies, commitment to life in the New World could be rather abstract or self-conscious ("We have to be Americans. We will be"); attachments to the Old World could, and no doubt did, draw on immigrants to an extent that was at times disorienting.[13] This is apparent even in that supposedly unambiguous celebration of assimilation of immigrant American Jewry: Mary Antin's *The Promised Land*. At the book's beginning, Antin observes that when she was growing up in Plotsk in Russian Poland, the destination of her father's business trips was described as a faraway, hostile place called Russia. Of course, Plotsk was part of the Russian empire. But not in the mind of this little girl. Plotsk was home: it was good, comfortable, and secure. And somewhere else was Russia: "Russia was the place where one's father went on business. It was so far-off, and so many bad things happened there." A disjuncture was drawn between good, nurturing local life and the venality of a larger, oppressive, and dangerous place.[14]

By and large, the glimpses of Eastern Europe in the imag-

inative work on immigrant Jewish life written in English at
the turn of the century almost exclusively depict its poverty
and pogroms. See, for instance, how Abraham Cahan's novel
The Rise of David Levinsky (a work of estimable girth that
describes in the greatest detail the clothing and building
trades of turn-of-the-century New York) dispenses with his
hero's Russian Jewish background, his childhood and adolescence, with a rare efficiency in some eighty pages.[15] This is all
the more striking since Cahan builds his novel around Levinsky's yearning for home. He intends his readers to feel
the poignancy of young Levinsky's encounter immediately
after his arrival in the United States when he is asked: "'And
what is your occupation? You have no trade, have you?' 'I read
Talmud,' I said confusedly. 'I see, but that's no business in
America.'"[16] Values of old and new worlds are contrasted
here. Yet Cahan does nothing further with the encounter and
doesn't build on it to compare, for instance, the cerebral
values of Levinsky's native Jewish Lithuania with the hurly-
burly of materialistic America. Quite the opposite, he shows
Levinsky's chief failing as an inability to move beyond such
preoccupations, which in Cahan's view are little more than
exercises in self-indulgence. Levinsky's preoccupation with
his dead mother (killed on the streets of Vilna by hostile Gentiles) intrudes on all his relations with women. His yearning
in America for a college education stops him from savoring
his considerable business success. This book—invoked today mostly as a sturdy immigrant melodrama—is, above all,
a splendid study of the inability to marshal one's desires.[17]

This preoccupation with hometown (its sounds, its synagogues, even its women) is itself a sign of malaise, a pathology at the core of the book. All is transformed by Levinsky
into abstraction: America too, as Levinsky tells it, "lured

me . . . chiefly, as [a land] of mystery, of fantastic experiences, of marvelous transformations." [18] Eastern Europe is of little importance here: it is merely a noisome, violent, pogrom-ridden backdrop, a place from which to escape.

Intimations of what Eastern Europe would later represent can be seen more clearly, I think, in Hutchins Hapgood's *The Spirit of the Ghetto*, published in 1902. Both books sought to explain an immigrant community much in the news at the time because of the business success of some rich Jews—hence the attention lavished by Cahan in his book on the mechanics of the Jewish trades in New York, where he seeks to clarify the commercial talents of Jews. Hapgood, a sympathetic non-Jewish journalist, sought to deflect attention from the economic achievements of the few visible rich immigrants by concentrating on those who personified, as he saw it, the true spirit of the East Side: its scholars, writers, and intellectuals. [19]

The book is an expansive, generous apologetic: the grasping, materialistic immigrant of popular culture, that immigrant captured vividly in Jacob Riis's famous 1890 report, is transformed. Ludlow Street meant for Riis the epitome of naked, unadorned materialism. [20] In contrast, Hapgood examines the faces of old, exhausted men behind sewing machines and sees scholars from the Old World: men who are "highly trained and educated," who uncannily resemble the learned, shrewd patriarchs captured by Rembrandt himself. "There are few more pathetic sights than an old venerable face—a man who had been perhaps a Hebraic or Talmudic scholar in the old country, carrying or pressing piles of coats in the melancholy sweat-shop." Hapgood sits in East Side cafes and admires its poets, translators, and formidable intellectuals who seek to sustain an East European legacy. This is the "spirit of the ghetto" (much the same ghetto that Irving Howe would rediscover half a century later), nurtured in Russia and sustained laboriously in the United States, a rich, fragile, embattled scholarly terrain.[21]

Still, this quintessential, spiritually attuned Jewish temperament traceable to Eastern Europe (and, as many would later argue, unable to master the vicissitudes of this world precisely because it is so adept at matters of the spirit), this "prince of the ghetto" who comes to be so much a part of the landscape of American Jewish life in the 1950s, was barely visible in Hapgood's time.[22] Hapgood's book must be read as a warmhearted exercise in subversion with its portrayal of East European Jewry posed as a counterweight to regnant stereotypes.

For the children of those who had participated in the mass immigration that began in the 1870s and continued until the changes in American immigration laws in 1921 and 1924, notions of the East European Jewish past were, to be sure, widely variegated. Yet, as Deborah Dash Moore astutely observes, it was immigration, not Eastern Europe, that constituted the (often remote) historical backdrop to their lives: "The concept of a second generation inevitably suggests a first generation, whose coherence developed around a pivotal event. Immigration serves as the point of reference; it defines an entire generation whose lives were reshaped by the experience. The children of immigrants, however, relate only indirectly to that point of reference."[23] For many second-generation American Jews, their European past was little more than a matter of indifference or, when pondered, distaste: a language unused, an accent (hopefully) shed, a medley of rejected attitudes toward money, clothes, sex, or food. Their often conflated East European and immigrant past was for children of his generation, as Irving Howe puts it, little

24

more than something that "clings to your skin, your speech, your nose" and inspires, in turn, dreams of universalism.[24]

But cling it often did. Especially in those circles inspired by left-wing politics, where Russia was at the center of concerns, the Russian past was integrated into visions of a shared future for immigrants and their children alike. Kazin recalls the socialism of his youth (in his sometimes suspiciously lyrical memoir, *A Walker in the City*) as an antidote to loneliness, as one long, convivial, quintessentially Russian Friday night songfest: socialism was "one long Friday night around the samovar and the cut-glass laden with nuts and fruits, all of us singing Tsuzamen, tsuzamen, ale tsuzamen! Then the heroes of the Russian novel—our kind of people—would walk the world and I—still wearing a circle-necked Russian blouse à la Tolstoy—would live forever with those I loved in that beautiful Russian country of the mind."[25] Irving Howe proposes, half-seriously, that his generation recognized Dostoevskian atmospherics in their experiences at home. He tells how Isaac Rosenfeld once insisted to him with mock solemnity that Chekhov wrote in Yiddish and that his English translator, in an effort to make him respectable, had falsified the record. Anyone with half an ear, stated Rosenfeld, could detect the Yiddish in Chekhov, in his sadness, absurdity, and humanism.[26]

An intriguing way to examine the transformation in regnant images of Eastern Europe from the 1920s until the 1950s is to trace the representation of the Old World in the fiction of Anzia Yezierska. Despite the repetitiveness that is her trademark, the place she evokes in the 1950s differs strikingly from that evoked in her better-known, early work.[27] In *Hungry Hearts* (1920), *Bread Givers* (1925), and also her novel of the 1930s, *All I Could Never Be,* Russian Poland is little more than a place of pogroms and brutal military conscription.

Shtetls There and Here

The protagonist's mother in *Bread Givers* speaks of a beautiful tablecloth she left behind, its beauty all the more vivid against the sordid, colorless backdrop of their immigrant lives: "There ain't in America such beautiful things like we had at home," she declares. The intensity with which she describes her lost treasure prompts her daughter to ask why she left Europe. Why did she not remain behind with the splendid tablecloth? The answer is simple and fierce: "Because the Tsar of Russia! Worms should eat him! He wanted for himself free soldiers to make pogroms. He wanted to make him a common soldier—to drink vodka with the drunken mouzhiks, eat pig, and shoot the people." [28]

In *Bread Givers*, Yezierska probes relations between a young Jewish woman and her father—a brutal, scholarly patriarch who is unwilling (no doubt, unable) to adapt himself to America and who expects his wife and daughters to satisfy his needs. ("He rushed from me, slamming the door, a defeated prophet, a Jeremiah to whom the people would not listen.") [29] In an uncomprehending immigrant milieu, his learning is little more than an expression of narcissism, indifference toward those with whom he lives. Here his inability to adapt has no bearing on the prospects facing his daughter, except for the haunting, crippling legacy he leaves her in demeaning her attempts to better herself. Her stubbornness may well have been inherited from him, but little else.

In contrast, there is a significant change in tone in Yezierska's 1950 fictionalized autobiography, *Red Ribbon on a White Horse*, where the relationship with her father remains a central theme. After years of literary obscurity in the wake of a flurry of attention in the 1920s, Yezierska insists on the similarity between her values and her father's bookish, Old World ones. These standards, to be sure, wrought havoc with her life, and, as she sees it, had she been different and embraced a good marriage or lucrative career, she could have lived comfortably and usefully in America. Instead, she lived like a hermit, obsessive and self-absorbed: "I turned to my writing the first thing in the morning and the last thing at night—as Father had turned to his prayers."[30]

In short, *Red Ribbon on a White Horse* is a study in conflicting definitions of success. The first is American, brash, fluent rather than profound, with the accumulation of wealth as its main criterion. The second is poor in worldly things but rich in spirit, awkward and ungainly but with these as trademarks of its superiority. The first is nurtured in the vacuous, self-absorbed New World; the second, its mirror image, is shaped by the values of Eastern Europe.

In Yezierska's novel of the 1950s, then, the standard contrasts of the second-generation American Jewish novel (Old World, New World; European, American; parochial, universal) are reconfigured. It is the Old World that emerges as a standard for sustained intelligence, spirit, and decency. In *Red Ribbon on a White Horse*, this culture's treatment of women—shabby, in earlier accounts, according to Yezierska—is barely noted; its antisemitism, too, is passed over without much comment. It is, rather, a source of pedigree for an American Jewish writer seeking solace in East European roots.

In this respect, Yezierska charts new ground late in life. She moves beyond the exoticism of immigrant existence at the core of her writings in the 1920s, which (much like the work of Michael Gold, Samuel Ornitz, and Daniel Fuchs), despite its gendered preoccupations, was built around discrete, predictable themes: an ambivalence toward a frayed, immigrant milieu that clings but no longer binds, that provides little more than a dash of color missing in the larger, anonymous world, an obsession with immigrant mother, and fear of father. Alfred Kazin sums up the limitations of this literature nicely: "The real drama behind most Jewish novels and plays, even when they are topical and revolutionary in feeling, is the contrast between the hysterical tenderness of the Oedipal relations and the 'world'; in the beginning there was the Jewish mother and her son, but her son grew up, he went out into the world, he became a writer. That was the beginning of his career, and usually the end of the novel."[31]

In the same years, in the late 1940s and 1950s, the poet and short-story writer Delmore Schwartz, like Yezierska, began to link his own claims for otherworldly poetic idealism to the otherworldliness in his ancestors, the Jews of Eastern Europe. In the story "The World Is a Wedding," he has the intellectual Israel Brown visit his student Edmund Kish, and introduced to Kish's East European–born mother, the erudite Jewish professor "spoke with her with customary pace and passion, telling her about her generation, the generation which came to America from Eastern Europe between 1890 and 1914. He spoke of the causes of the departure of this generation from the old world, the problems and tricks of the ocean liner agencies, the prospects of immigrants, the images of the new world which had inhabited their minds."[32] As he left, Mrs. Kish breathed a sigh of relief. Edmund turns to his mother and says, "You have just seen a genius." Her reply: "How much money does he make?" This sentence, says one of the novella's characters soon afterward, is "one of the most heart-breaking sentences of our time."[33] Back in Eastern Europe, he means to tell us, such things did not occur, such base notions weren't thought in a place where Judaism was characterized by unworldly and selfless women and men, guided by the teachings of a splendid, humane lore. "I am proud of my ancestors," declares a character of Schwartz's in another

Shtetls There and Here

story, who identifies himself as of "Russian-Jewish detrac-
tion": "My ancestors, in whom I take pride, were scholars,
poets, prophets and students of God when most of Europe
worshipped sticks and stones: not that I hold that against any
of you, it is not your fault that your forebears were barbarians
grovelling and groping about for peat or something."[34]

What began to change in the 1950s in such perceptions
about the Jewish past is the resurrection of East European
Jewish life as a counterweight to America. There was now, of
course, a greater distance separating American Jews from
Eastern Europe, which encouraged, among other responses,
a heightened sentimentality. In this regard, the impact of the
Holocaust on attitudes toward Eastern Europe remains difficult to assess. Deborah E. Lipstadt states that the European
catastrophe didn't emerge until the 1960s as "a factor in the
construct of American Jewish identity": "From the end of the
war until the 1960s, a 'can-do,' optimistic spirit pervaded
America. . . . Americans were engaged in obtaining goods
and achieving goals that they never had before and, in many
cases, never dreamt would be theirs, e.g., college educations,
homes, cars, and televisions. . . . It did not seem to be an appropriate time to focus on a painful past, particularly a past
which seemed to be of no direct concern to this country."[35]

Lipstadt describes accurately, no doubt, the most readily
observed reactions of American Jews, which are not incon-
sistent with other, less transparent, less publicly manifest
responses. These may have included attempts (as Lipstadt
herself, fleetingly, admits) to extract a message of some sort
from the fate of European Jewry; the use to which Anne
Frank was put is an indication of such an effort. American
Jews might have been particularly motivated to recast the
East European Jewish past in nostalgic terms as part of an
effort to say something coherent about this now-obliterated

29

world in the terms available to them: sentimental rather than commemorative or horrified.[36] As Irving Howe recalls: "I cannot prove a connection between the Holocaust and the turn to Jewish themes in American fiction, at first urgent and quizzical, later fashionable and manipulative. I cannot prove that my own turn to Yiddish literature during the fifties was due to the shock following the war years. But it would be foolish to scant the possibility."[37]

Eastern Europe was increasingly used in Jewish literature in the United States as a chastisement (as in Yezierksa and Delmore Schwartz) or, improbable as this might seem, as proof for continuity, a reassurance that things Jewish hadn't really changed much. Influencing this, it would seem, was the Holocaust, which rendered Eastern Europe more conducive to sentimentalization, the appearance of identity as a category on the American cultural scene, which shifted Jewish self-understanding considerably, and, in rather less obvious ways, the suburbanization of the American middle class.

By the early 1950s, both the Jewish past in Russia and the texture of life in immigrant communities in the United States were suddenly matters of intellectual interest, as Norman Podhoretz noted. (He was then a young literary scholar sending his first pieces to *Commentary*.) Podhoretz found this cheering, if puzzling; perhaps, he suggested, it was prompted by a longing for a cultural intimacy similar to that exemplified by the contemporaneous postwar rediscovery of Walt Whitman, less for his talent than for the quintessential Americanness of his voice.[38]

There was ample proof for this turn in attitudes: Podhoretz made these observations in his review of the splendid collection of Yiddish stories edited by Irving Howe and Eliezer Greenberg (which appeared in 1954). Podhoretz also pointed to the newfound popularity of Martin Buber's Hasidic tales and to the more or less concurrent publication of the Howe / Greenberg anthology and of the anthropological account of shtetl culture *Life Is with People*. A popular (now forgotten) revue *The World of Sholom Aleichem* was then on Broadway; a revival of Peretz followed soon after, this time off-Broadway. Podhoretz did not mention that this interest was now curiously disassociated from Russia. By the 1950s, the fears engendered by McCarthyism discouraged such a linkage. This, in turn, may have further encouraged the depiction of a discretely Jewish terrain, the shtetl, that small Jewish town celebrated (with neither particular acumen nor accuracy) in the 1952 book *Life Is with People*, which served the producers of *Fiddler on the Roof* as an authoritative source.[39]

Isaac Bashevis Singer's transformation in the 1950s and 1960s from a complex, introspective, and little-known writer into a wildly celebrated, "simple, old-fashioned sprite" illustrates much the same pattern. The Americanization of his image was, arguably, even more influential than his work. Singer's literary genesis has been skillfully studied by Janet Hadda in a biography that examines how he himself managed to remake the Yiddish writer Bashevis into the American Singer, that "chronicler of an ethnographically informative, crude, colorful world." Hadda writes, "Bashevis had correctly, if intuitively, perceived that for readers of English, an Eastern European Jew had to be old-fashioned, mildmannered, even naive in order to be believable."[40]

She shows that by the time he was awarded the Nobel Prize, in 1978, the Prize committee, as well as much of the press in the United States and elsewhere, had ceased to read Singer in anything but the most banal terms: "No one had the slightest interest in Bashevis, the immigrant genius, the former enfant terrible turned world-weary Jeremiah. The press and electronic media resonated with the idea that this prize commemorated the work of a homespun and humble soul who had faithfully represented the beautiful but tragic world of a moral and pious society that had been cruelly extinguished by the Nazi Holocaust."[41] Hence, it was his few passing quips, mostly the cute, impish moments of his Nobel Prize speech, that were reported in the *New York Times*; the *Washington Post* explained to its readers that Singer captured that world "known to American readers through 'Fiddler on the Roof.'"[42] A fiercely competitive, self-aware, experimental stylist was transformed into a humble chronicler of a flattened shtetl.

Interestingly, Singer was among the first Jewish writers in America to imagine a direct, even linear relationship for Jews between the East European shtetl and the American suburb. This motif would emerge as a significant—and, possibly, even a central—feature of American Jewish writing in the 1960s and 1970s. His eerily cheerful saga "The Little Shoemakers," written in 1945, and its contemporaneous analogue, the dark, deservedly better known "Gimpel the Fool" (both set in fictional Frampol), show different sides of the same naive soul. In "The Little Shoemakers," a humble cobbler from Chmielnicki's murderous Ukraine (so recently, of course, the site of Nazi horrors, which aren't mentioned in the story) in his last years joins his children in the New Jersey suburbs, where they have become substantial shoe manufacturers. The sons set the near-mute greenhorn in his own workshop, a meticulous reproduction of his humble place of business in Frampol, where he—and they, too—sit, sing, and labor over their ancestral trade. "No, praise God, they had not become idolators in Egypt. . . . The old man rattled and bumbled deep in his chest, and suddenly, began to sing in a stifled, hoarse voice."[43]

The American revival of interest in the shtetl is best demonstrated, of course, by the Broadway play, later the film, *Fiddler on the Roof. Fiddler* was originally designed to celebrate shtetl life in still happier terms than is apparent even from the finished, amiable product; the shtetl, its producers wished to signal, was superior somehow to America (though for reasons that, no doubt, eluded them). Still, the comparison remained a central theme of the play. As librettist Joseph Stein recalled: "We had a scene which lasted up to the opening in Detroit in which Tevye read a letter from his brother-in-law in America. It was an amusing scene, and it led to a song called 'Letters from America' or 'Anatevka' in which the people sang of how very happy they were about being in Anatevka. 'America may sound fine but we are very, very happy in Anatevka.'"[44]

The play made its first appearance on Broadway in 1964. Sholem Aleichem, whose work inspired it, was the most popular of Yiddish writers, but to translate the dexterous, anxious wordplay of the original Yiddish onto the American stage presented a considerable challenge which the producers never tried to meet. Critics were disappointed. ("The cutest shtetl we've never had," Irving Howe quipped in a review.)[45] The play's creators admitted after its stupendous reception that they had feared it might be "too serious and too Jewish and a disaster." As one remembered: "As a matter of fact, one of the reasons we did it ourselves was that I couldn't conceive of going to a producer and saying, 'We have this idea of a show about a lot of Jews in Russia. You know they have a pogrom and get thrown out of their village.'"[46] Far from disaster, it would be one of the great success stories of

American theater and it would define for American Jews, more so than any other cultural artifact of the 1960s and beyond, the content of their Jewish past.

No doubt, there are many reasons for the success of *Fiddler*. Tevye himself, who has declaimed the need for "Tradition" in dozens of languages, offers many different things to audiences in America, and elsewhere. (I first saw the film version during a research trip in Helsinki in the late 1970s and the audience there loved it.) Still, I look here at the play in terms of its representation of community. "For me," recalled Stein, "community was always central to the story."[47]

This is all the more apparent when the play is examined alongside another important text dating from the same period: the short story by Philip Roth "Eli, the Fanatic." Both seek to explore the brightest and the darkest aspects of Jewish community life. The story is set in postwar suburban America, the play in turn-of-the-century Russia, but both are inspired by similar concerns: the building of community (an overriding concern in an increasingly suburban postwar America) and the preoccupation with family, father, and continuity.

Of course, the tales are, on the most obvious level, quite different. Tevye is meant to reassure, to provide his audience with a promise of continuity. In contrast, "Eli, the Fanatic," is among the first significant pieces of fiction written by an American Jewish writer in the English language that discusses the Nazi catastrophe; it is a tale of darkness, alienation, perhaps insanity. But, then, these same juxtapositions are implicit in much of the widely discussed literature on suburbia written in the 1950s and 1960s, which itself veers between these extremes, the one serving as a warning or litmus test for the other. Is the shtetl an intrusive or an inspiring presence?

Shtetls There and Here

In *Fiddler* the audience is reassured that Jews carry the shtetl with them, and this promises a healthy dose of sanity and good sense. In "Eli, the Fanatic," the same legacy haunts; it means perpetuating traits inconceivable for a Jewish pact with the suburbs. The dark legacy of the shtetl here is the reason for alienation, a key to that perplexing dilemma in American cultural life in the 1950s. In both, images of suburbia—itself, of course a fractured, widely variegated experience and very different for Jews in Van Nuys and those in New Rochelle—are the backdrop, whether explicitly or not. Shtetl is, alternately, an inspiration or a dybbuk.

Although the themes, the names of characters, bits of dialogue, and plot structure in *Fiddler on the Roof* were inspired by Sholem Aleichem, these were wholly remade. What emerged, as the play's author, Richard Altman, saw it, was a study of "a man's need to change with the times." The show, says Altman, "follows a downhill path, as first the traditions and then the stability of Tevye's peasant village are eroded and undermined."[48] Tevye, he writes, is a "man in the state of transition." Or, as lyricist Sheldon Harnick recalled: "And [choreographer Jerome Robbins] kept asking the same question: 'What's it about? What's it about?' I don't know which one of us finally said it. But someone said, 'Do you know what this play is about? It's about the dissolution of a way of life. . . . And that was the beginning of 'Tradition.'"[49]

Curiously, the fiddler in the title role—the show's emblem of tradition, perched predictably on Chagall's roof—is all but absent (the original actor in the role, a distinguished violinist, nearly quit in frustration because of his progressively dwindling lines).[50] What was left of him, after various rewrites, was an elusive, vague reminder of a tradition whose hold on Tevye himself is elastic, at best. The fiddler follows

Shtetls There and Here

Tevye to America: there can be little doubt who will there call the tune.

In *Fiddler*, Tevye is the father of all of us, or so the authors affirm; fittingly, the script is dedicated "to our fathers." He is not meant necessarily to be emulated (what Old World father is?), but Tevye's foremost concerns—his children, their marriages, his role in a mostly female world, negotiating life in a Gentile milieu, building and sustaining community, the wages of prestige ("If I were a rich man . . .")—also figure among the chief concerns of postwar, suburban Jewry. Tevye represents patriarchy at its most lovable, flexible, and pragmatic. It is only when confronted with the marriage of his youngest daughter to a Gentile that he finds it impossible to adapt tradition to contemporary demands. Only then does tradition intrude rather than amuse: "Here in Anatevka, we have traditions for everything—how to eat, how to sleep, how to wear clothes." Gemeinschaft here is sweet, warm, unintrusive. At the play's end, Tevye moves on to a new place— to America, naturally; in Sholem Aleichem's fictional work, his destination is the Land of Israel.[51] He will adapt himself easily; that much is certain. He comes endowed, we're assured, with the requisite skills.

In contrast, just a few years earlier when, in 1942, the skilled popularizer of Jewish culture Maurice Samuel published *The World of Sholom Aleichem*, the first significant book that sought to resurrect the Yiddish writer's work for an American audience, none of these themes were given prominence. The difference in emphasis between this book of the 1940s and *Fiddler* is revealing.[52]

There is, indeed, a striking similarity between the central concerns of *Fiddler on the Roof* and those in the vast literature about suburbia produced in the 1950s and early 1960s:

Shtetls There and Here

William Whyte's brilliant broadside *The Organization Man* with his warnings about the suburban male commuter who loses all, including his soul; David Riesman's dark reflections on "suburban sadness," a flattened world outside the city without fathers, privacy, or individuality; the 1961 novel *Revolutionary Road*, which tells us that in the suburbs there are "no looming shadows, and no gaunt silhouettes. It was invincibly cheerful, a toyland of white and pastel houses."[53]

For Jews, the postwar suburbs were among the first American places of residence where they were compelled to give widespread thought to the building of communal life. Earlier, except for the relatively small numbers of Jews living in small towns, most Jews clustered in America's largest cities, where they tended to live in neighborhoods that they dominated demographically as well as culturally. Demands for Jewish organizational life in the city were less pressing, money was typically scarce, and the presence of Gentiles (mostly of lesser status) constituted in itself little motivation for the launching of religious or other communal institutions. Although a good many American synagogues that were still functioning well into the 1960s and later were built in the decade or so prior to the Great Depression, the building spurt of postwar, suburban Jewry was essentially without precedent.

In suburbia, substantial numbers of American Jews now lived, often for the first time, in places where Gentiles were in the majority. They had moved from ethnic communities in the cities to new enclaves defined largely by status. As a result, Jewish life in suburbia was an issue at the top of the communal agenda. As a social scientist at the time summed up the central preoccupations of suburban life, these included "the breakup of older communities where social identity was relatively fixed and . . . the mass movement into new communities (e.g. suburbs) where new sources of social identity had to be created." [54] Here in dry, sociological terminology we find an adequate, uninspiring synopsis of what the authors of *Fiddler on the Roof* did to make Tevye palatable —and refreshingly relevant—on Broadway: Tevye is made over into a guide to elusive patriarchy, the loosening bonds of family, faith, and community. As improbable as this sounds, suburban life is much like the shtetl of old—or so we are told. "You can take the Jew out of the shtetl," wrote Sol Gittleman in still another book of the 1970s devoted to images of family in Jewish literature, "but . . . you could not take the shtetl out of the Jew." [55] In *Fiddler* this is a message of comfort; in Philip Roth's "Eli, the Fanatic," it is precisely this that haunts the hapless Eli Peck.

Peck is soon to be a father ("I'm the father" are his last words before, at the story's end, he is carted off by hospital attendants and drugged).[56] At the story's beginning, he is a local, civic-minded attorney hired to dislodge a yeshiva made up of Holocaust survivors that has taken up residence in his suburb. The yeshiva employs an apparently mute Hasid, scarred irreparably by the Nazis, dressed in traditional garb with a large hat and capote, whose walks in the town have Jews in an uproar. On his first encounter with Tzuref, the wily yeshiva head, Peck arrives straight from the train station, drained and vulnerable after a long commute: "He was not feeling as professional as usual—the place was too dim, it was too late." [57] After a few moments in an uncomfortable chair facing this Holocaust survivor, Peck deflates (he has a history of nervous breakdowns), his professional bearing escapes him, his briefcase weighs him down, he finds himself drawn, unwittingly, toward Tzuref and, in particular, to the other man, the Hasid in the hat, his mute double, with his dead children, a refugee from murdered communities that cannot be replaced by status-conscious, pleasure-seeking Woodenton. The Hasid, whose hat and suit Peck will eventually put on to greet his wife and his newborn son, came, as Tzuref describes it, from "[a] village full of friends? A synagogue where you knew the feel of every seat under your pants? Where with your eyes closed you could smell the cloth of the Torah?"[58]

In contrast, Eli lives in a place that espouses moderation, a "progressive suburban community," as his letter to Tzuref states, "whose members both Jewish and Gentile, are anxious that their families live in comfort and beauty and serenity."[59] Woodenton, in its prosperity, calm, and safety is, as Eli tells himself, precisely the sort of place for which his grandparents in Poland had risked their lives. Now Jews had a place where families were safe and, perhaps, he muses, it is necessary to protect such a blessing with toughness and numbness. He stares at the town's apricot-colored houses, anticipates the birth of his firstborn, dons the suit of a Hasid, and is carried away at the story's end drugged yet unsedated. "In a moment they tore off his jacket—it gave so easily, in one yank. Then a needle slid under his skin. The drug calmed his soul, but it did not touch it down where the blackness had reached."[60] Throughout there is this same juxtaposition of black and white: blackness as the unlikely representation of the moral purity of the Old World set against the backdrop of a new world that is bright, self-absorbed, and irredeemably vacuous.

~ 2 ~

Reinventing Heders

Depending on our interests, we carry with us different bits and pieces of this complex whole. The parent "knows" of a bygone age in which manners were strict and children domesticated. The sociologist "knows" of an urban culture largely immune to anarchic challenge and sudden gusts of violence. The religious man and the moralists "know" of a lost epoch of agreed values. Each of us can summon up appropriate vignettes: of the well-ordered household, with its privacies and domestics; of the Sunday parks, leisured and safe; of Latin in the schoolroom and apostolic finesse in the college quad; of real bookstores and literate parliamentary debate. . . . It is against their remembrance of that great summer, and our own symbolic knowledge of it, that we test the present cold.

— George Steiner, *In Bluebeard's Castle*

Chaim Weizmann recalls his school days in his autobiography, *Trial and Error*: "Like all Jewish boys, I went to cheder, beginning at the age of four. Like nearly all cheders, mine was a squalid, one-room school. . . . If my cheder differed from the others, it was perhaps in the possession of a family goat which took shelter with us in cold weather. And if my first Rebbi, or teacher, differed from the others it was in the degree of his pedagogical incompetence."[1] Warm evocations of heders were rare. Few who recalled with pleasure other aspects of the East European Jewish past remembered heders happily. Even Abraham Cahan's hapless, rich David Levinsky, as discussed in the previous chapter, who remembers with fondness other aspects of his lost Lithuanian hometown (a symptom of his pathology, as Cahan sees it), speaks of his melamed as a sadist seeking pleasure from the torture of his boys.[2]

"A classroom filled with death," said the leading early-nineteenth-century Jewish Enlightenment thinker Isaac Ber Levinsohn of the traditional Jewish primary school in which the majority of East European Jewish boys between the ages of three or four and twelve were educated in Bible and liturgy. Heder children are like sheep led to the slaughter—this is how Mendele Mocher Seforim puts it. Shimon Dubnow, in his first published essay, in the newspaper *Russkii evrei* in 1880, describes heders in his hometown Mstislavl

Reinventing Heders

thusly: "A crime is committed there: the massacre of young innocents."[3]

Critics were unrelenting—no doubt, little constrained in their criticisms of heders since these were privately run institutions outside the official hegemony of Jewish communal life and, hence, all the more vulnerable. The schools' curriculum typically was deemed dreadful, its teachers untrained, its physical conditions unsanitary. Critics, especially maskilim, the self-consciously enlightened Jews who saw education as central to the campaign for the transformation of East European Jewish life, viewed the heder teacher as an outstanding foe. Indeed, even the religious journalist Eliezer Meir Lipschutz—in a rare, empathetic portrait of the institution—admits that in traditional circles the word "melamed" came to be synonymous in the early twentieth century with *batlan* (wastrel). He complements his study of heders in Eastern Europe with a sampling of better-known melamed jokes, all of them popular among religious Jews (e.g., If all else fails, you can kill yourself or become a melamed, and the former is preferable.)[4]

This bleak portrait was given a scientific, empirical scaffolding in work by medical investigators. Widely disseminated first in 1903 (though studies by doctors of the hygienic shortcomings of heders had appeared in Russian as early as 1879), reports on the heder described it as a dangerous place on medical grounds. The Russian Society for the Protection of National Health examined heders in the Moldavanka neighborhood of Odessa, one of the poorer parts of the city. They found that, despite the area's poverty, mortality of Jewish boys up to five years of age was half that of the city as a whole. However, mortality among heder boys of the same neighborhood aged five to ten was, they asserted, double the national average. The long hours children were compelled to languish in stuffy, badly ventilated rooms (eight to nine hours daily), their poverty, and their lack of activity precipitated, in the words of the report, "illness and death."[5] True or not, the statistics were widely believed at the time to be accurate.

Much the same alarming pattern was found in the city of Kharkov, and these findings were published in 1908 in the new Jewish scientific journal *Evreiskii meditsinskii golos*. Written by a fieldworker for the Society for the Promotion of Enlightenment among Jews (Obshchestvo dlia rasprostraneniia prosvescheniia mezhdu evreiami v Rossii; OPE), this copiously documented report provided data on the number of windows in local heders, their furnishings, measurements of the students, etc. Heders here were deemed guilty of denying children "air, light, or activity" and they trampled on lives with a scientifically proven regularity.[6]

Still more comprehensive—and no less scathing—is *Sovremennyi kheder* (The contemporary heder), a hundred-page book written by fieldworkers of OPE that surveyed the institution with the help of questionnaires as well as visits by inspectors to hundreds of schools in various parts of the Pale of Settlement and Poland. It found that of the ninety-five melameds examined in Ekaterinoslav province, for instance, twenty-three said that they occasionally read a book; seventy-two never did. Not that they were engrossed in holy script: the majority of Ekaterinoslav melameds surveyed could not translate a biblical text accurately. So little Jewish history was taught in heders that many students surveyed in the provinces of New Russia (which included Ekaterinoslav) did not know of the existence of a Second Temple, let alone its destruction. Despite the fact that only twenty-nine of the approximately one hundred children surveyed in Ekaterinoslav heders spoke Yiddish at home (a very low number compared with other regions of the Pale of Settlement but unsurprising in this highly Russified area), heder instruction in that province, as elsewhere, was typically in Yiddish, further testimony to the inflexibility of the heder curriculum. Most melameds were old and few even read newspapers. In the Ukrainian town of Zhitomir, eight out of the ninety melameds queried about their reading habits admitted that (sometimes) they read a book. Even here, in a milieu reputed to be more Jewishly stable and literate than Ekaterinoslav, "the melamed who knows no [Hebrew] grammar is a pathetic feature of our daily life."[7]

The worst school in the Ukraine was in Rovno, insisted one of the inspectors. Twenty boys were crammed into a dimly lit room with three tiny windows. The same room served as a *hekdesh*, a combination poorhouse and hospice, where the indigent or sick paid three to five kopecks for daily lodging. The voices of the melamed and his wife were rasping and unusually unpleasant. Without restraint, she called out to him throughout the day, interrupting lessons. "I left this heder shattered physically and spiritually," writes the inspector.[8]

It is all the more surprising, therefore, that at the turn of the century, when the heder appeared to be at its most vulnerable, it was increasingly spoken about (and by consciously modern Jews, too) with endearment. The phenomenon bemused the editors of *Sovremennyi kheder*, who observed that in New Russia, where heders were more out of touch with everyday social reality than anywhere else in the empire, there was a new, jarring appreciation for the same schools as providing a "uniquely Jewish atmosphere."[9]

Its critics sounded sentimental, and, curiously, uneasy about the prospect of facing the future without them. Literary critic Dan Miron has observed a similar unease with other changes in maskilic circles in Eastern Europe, especially at those moments when otherwise long awaited changes finally seemed to occur: "We see this most distinctly when [maskilim] comment on the actual changes which the cultural behavior of Eastern European Jewry was undergoing before their very eyes; changes which they themselves propagated and celebrated. One realizes that this celebration almost always leaves [them with] a bitter aftertaste."[10] Such reactions underline how essentially conservative the Russian Haskalah (Enlightenment) was in its desire to reemploy fundamental Judaic principles (as it saw them) in the construction of what it hoped would be a stable Jewish modernity.

It is in this context that the conversations on the heder that I analyze in this chapter should be considered. The support for heders and talmud-torahs that we will encounter was rooted in the widespread belief that they were nearing the end of their natural lives and that their loss would leave an insurmountable gap. This is what was meant by the designation of such schools as "national" institutions. The term *natsionalnaia evreiskaia shkola* (national Jewish school) was widely used in connection with support for heders on "nationalist" grounds, a common motif across the cultural and ideological spectrum of Russian Jewry. The schools, it is true, remained strikingly popular; five-sixths of all Jewish boys in Russia and Poland still attended them at the turn of the century, but, as was often noted, for increasingly shorter stints, typically adding up to no more than two to three years.

What the word "national" meant (for many of the participants in these discussions, at any rate) was "basically Jewish." In other words, heders and talmud-torahs were widely believed to be uniquely suited to checking the cultural slippage of young Jews, a major theme in Russian Jewish life at the time and all the more ominous in light of the apparent vulnerability of the heder.

Especially striking about these discussions is the relative absence of sectarian, political struggle. No single political group dominated them (although this is precisely how, as we'll see, the Zionist-inspired literature on school reform spoke about this episode). Rather, they were the product of a wide-ranging, extensive effort that traversed the otherwise fractious cultural and political divide of fin de siècle Russian Jewish life.

There were differences over details, of course. More interesting, though, was the consensus on basic issues. If, in retrospect, it is the differences that have loomed largest in the existing secondary literature (differences over the preferred language of instruction, curriculum, the advisability of reforming the heder and talmud-torah, etc.), these were dwarfed at the time because it was argued that the disappearance of traditional Jewish primary schools would harm Jews far more than would their continued existence. Fear of their extinction and of the (potentially dangerous) chasm that would be left overwhelmed the considerable distaste felt for them.

Increasingly, heders represented something of a litmus test for authenticity in Russian Jewish life, bulwarks in a now fragmented Jewish culture that could, it was feared, collapse or at least greatly weaken without their inspiration: a dubious institution of great (and, at least, in the short run), unparalleled efficacy. The special value of the documentary sources on which this chapter is based—mostly the transcripts of teachers' meetings held between 1902 and 1904—is not the originality of their arguments. These are voices captured in the brisk protocol summaries produced for internal organizational use. The speakers are communal activists, schoolteachers, and directors in what are rather unmediated, raw, and, hence, surprisingly revealing exchanges.

The sources serve as still another reminder of how our current knowledge of Russian Jewry is severely restricted. What tended to enter the historical record (in Russia, perhaps, more so than elsewhere in modern Jewish life) was often the product of the most ideologically coherent groups. Thus, we have a history written by Zionists and, to a lesser extent, by Jewish socialists, a self-fulfilling historical record left by those who tended to airbrush their antagonists from the past with the sincerity, cunning, or innocence of political conviction.

These discussions should also remind us that, at the turn of the century, many secular as well as religious Russian Jews also doubted that their community could sustain itself in terms of what they saw as its essential qualities; the identity of these particular qualities was, of course, the subject of much debate. It is, however, the widespread anxiety itself that interests me here. The heder provided those Russian Jews whom we hear in these documents with the promise that it could contribute toward sustaining their culture in this moment of uncertainty, its otherwise much disparaged backwardness itself evidence of its sturdy, time-tested efficacy, its value as an institution of considerable, perhaps even unequaled worth.

Like other private, unregistered schools in Russia, heders existed for much of the nineteenth century in the shadows, with only sporadic government interference. In effect, melameds conducted their own affairs without the help of local Jewish communities or, after its founding in 1863, the empire's main communal body, the OPE. This situation began to change only in the 1890s with an easing of government restrictions on private education. After much debate (which lasted for the better part of a decade, until 1902), the OPE decided to add support for heders to its very short list of top institutional funding priorities.[11]

Heder reform now achieved a new Jewish communal visibility and it became one of the most contested issues in the Jewish press. In a rather typical issue of the Russian-language Jewish newspaper *Voskhod* in spring 1903, the lead article begins: "Questions regarding the reform of Jewish school affairs and . . . educating our children in a Jewish spirit agitate the contemporary Russian Jewish community." An article on the next page announces: "The question of national education preoccupies everyone's mind." Both are about heder reform and, in both, the term "national education" is used favorably—despite *Voskhod's* otherwise clearly stated antinationalist stance.[12]

Once these matters find their way into historical accounts of the period, however, heder reform is depicted in far more constrained terms—in fact, mostly in the context of the Zionist *heder metukan* (reformed heder). The movement promoting such schools was, indeed, impressive, and by 1903, perhaps as many as 900 Zionist schools were set up in Russia (10% of registered heders). They were inspired by the so-called natural system of Hebrew language, or *ivrit be-ivrit*, in which it was stressed that all classroom communication must be conducted in the ancient tongue.[13]

Reports by Zionists themselves of these efforts were, not surprisingly, upbeat, even triumphalist. I quote Hayyim Zuta's turn-of-the-century pamphlet, *Ha-melamed ve-ha-moreh* (The melamed and the teacher): "And now there has arrived a new epoch. The old melamed . . . is shrinking, dwindling. Because of hoary old age he cannot adapt to the

new situation and cannot manage to stand firm against
the new currents pulling at Jews. The new national teacher is
so different from the old melamed, so different in training,
in intellectual outlook, in attitude to life, in goals and aspirations. Without doubt the future belongs to this young
teacher." [14] In short, Zionists depicted the situation as a natural process of old age and disintegration, with youth taking
over where the old left off—a straightforward, cultural nationalist narrative with vigorous, youthful Zionist teachers
inheriting (without much strife) the mantle for the next generation. Even traditionalist critics of the institution—who,
by all accounts, waged a bitter battle against it—are written
off in this benevolent, positivist version of old age, death, and
renewal, with the Zionists as the natural beneficiaries of the
finest, albeit outdated, remnants of the past.

Zuta, later a prominent educator in Jewish Palestine and
the author of several textbooks used widely there, offers an
influential description in his memoirs, published in the mid-
1930s, of the origins of heder reform in Russia as a product of
Zionism and its impact. He describes at length the first meeting of Jewish primary school teachers sponsored by OPE,
held in Orsha near Vitebsk in Belorussia in spring 1902.
Brought together at the meeting for the first time were, in
Zuta's words, *leumim* and *mitbolelim* (nationalists and assimilationists). It was feared by Zuta's Zionist mentor, the
stolid, influential nationalist stalwart Menachem Mendel
Ussishkin, that the latter would win handily. Ussishkin urged
Zuta to attend the Orsha gathering. He predicted, gloomily,
that it would be little more than a benign get-together of
"teachers of mathematics and Russian," but he urged Zuta to
try to "storm the walls of the assimilationists." [15]

Zuta's depiction of the meeting affirms the soundness of
Ussishkin's fears. Most of the teachers who attended it, writes

Zuta, saw Jewish schools as vehicles for integration into Russian society, and their lamentable, liberal convictions could be summarized thusly: "[t]o prove that most important was the place where one resides, its life, its culture, its rich literature as an extension of the more general culture, European and worldwide. To the extent to which they even thought about the views of the nationalists, they attributed to them no value whatsoever; quite the contrary, they warned of their national chauvinism."[16] Nevertheless, outnumbered as nationalists were at Orsha, they were so persuasive that they managed to turn the gathering around: a happy, unexpected victory over terrible odds. Their plank won a comfortable majority. Zuta himself, together with a Zionist colleague, was called upon to produce a comprehensive curriculum for Jewish primary schools, which appeared, in Russian, the next year.

Quite an achievement—that is, if this is what occurred. There is reason to question much of this version. It is Zuta, in fact, who is responsible for inspiring these doubts. At the National Library in Jerusalem he deposited the only existing copy (this is how he describes it in his memoirs) of a forty-three-page Russian-language transcript of the Orsha meeting, a highly detailed summary by its recording secretary. Zuta himself, who mentions the document in his book, raises no question about its veracity. The title of the transcript is, in fact, in Zuta's hand, as is his note of dedication to the Jerusalem library.[17]

The transcript contradicts Zuta's published account, written some thirty years later, in nearly every respect. For instance, at the opening session held at the Orsha talmud-torah (a long, grueling session that broke at 2:30 A.M.), seventy-six people were recognized by the chair, often more than once. Chairing the session was a well-known local Zionist. From the very beginning, and contrary to Zuta's recollections, the meeting discussed almost exclusively the best strategies for "national" Jewish education. Only one speaker at the session —a well-known female school director named B. S. Ilion— made an antinationalist argument and insisted that schools must be international in character and should provide a general, humanistic education. Another speaker, Gershon Lifshits, expressed reservations about whether the Talmud should be taught in nationally oriented schools.[18]

Beginning with this first session and throughout the meeting, as the transcript makes clear, nationalism set the agenda. The discussions themselves were dominated entirely by nationalist categories, which, in turn, established the terms of reference for its very few critics. Hence, Ilion, in her criticisms of the *heder metukan*, proposed that "national values" were best inculcated through the teaching of history (the history of pogroms and oppression is how she put it), and not language.

There was much argument at Orsha, of course. However, much like Ilion's criticisms of the *heder metukan*, these disputes were mostly tactical, not substantive in character. The question most often asked was: how best to achieve a national education? Some insisted that practical skills should be taught, so that Jews would become more productive. Most argued that schools must provide students with a better sense of Judaism's "spirit": they must "educate" as well as "teach." By spirit, what was meant (as was made clear repeatedly) was national content, although its precise curricular identity was the source of considerable argument. Some expressed skepticism as to whether children in the *heder metukan* could be taught effectively in Hebrew, especially since so few East European Jews knew the language well enough to speak it. Only one participant at the Orsha meeting made a strong case for

Yiddish, not Hebrew. Discussions were wide-ranging: educational practices in Switzerland, Scotland, Ireland, and England were cited by participants—and sometimes evaluated at length—in an effort to locate concrete examples of national educational standards. These foreign referents seem to have been especially intriguing, it seems, for teachers seeking ways to teach Jewish values without a primary reliance on religious Judaism.[19]

The proceedings at Orsha resembled many other meetings on Jewish educational reform held in the same period. In 1904, for instance, a meeting was called to evaluate publicly an OPE report in which it was stated that "our communal-national schools" (i.e., talmud-torahs) must concern "the entire nation." Debate concentrated on how best to instill these values. Families, not schools, insisted one participant, do this most efficiently. Some supported Hebrew as an exemplary national tool; others made the case for Yiddish. Only one speaker urged that separate Jewish schools be discarded entirely, but he garnered no support and nothing further was said in support of the position. Especially revealing about this particular meeting was the way in which it subjected the various building blocks of nationalism to scrutiny and sought to distinguish between religion and nationalism, ethnicity, and nationality (*narodnost'*). Yiddish found more partisans than at the earlier meeting in Orsha. There was some disagreement on how best to infiltrate existing talmud-torahs and how to run other Jewish communal schools most efficiently.[20]

Once again, most telling about these discussions was what was not mentioned: there was no principled opposition to nationalism. Nationalism emerged as a consensual position despite the fact that, as a political movement (whether Zionist or Bundist), it had many opponents at the gathering. But in terms of educational discourse, at least, a national agenda appeared to have made the most sense. A further example, drawn from the transcript of an OPE meeting of its Odessa branch in 1903, are the remarks of Gershon Lifshits, which I reproduce from a transcript that includes two catcalls:

> I do not think that we must talk here about nationalist and religious education. (Dr. Landesman calls out: "All we do is talk about nationalism.") I wish to speak here only about the financial aspect of the [branch's annual] report. But several times this theme [of nationalism] has been touched upon, and I want to say something about it. Groundlessly, opponents of the [Odessa branch's] committee have appropriated for themselves the title "nationalists." We too are nationalists—in our own way and with our specific point of view. . . . Jewish subjects occupy a considerable part of the curriculum—by the way, former students of these schools work in my office and none know Hebrew, which doesn't detract at all from their being good Jews and excellent employees. I too was educated in the rabbinical seminaries.[21]

The text meanders off in the direction of financial concerns. Lifshits was the first speaker at the meeting following a long, authoritative pronouncement by the ideologue Ahad Ha'am (pen name for Asher Ginsberg), whom he sought to criticize. The distance between the quality of their remarks is, indeed, stark; still, the apparent incoherence of Lifshits's argument shouldn't obscure how he manages, at one and the same time, to oppose the OPE's leading nationalists while refusing to disassociate himself from what he insists on calling nationalism.

Later, at the same meeting, Lifshits showed himself to be

sufficiently supportive of Jewish nationalism, as he understood it, to applaud an OPE plank calling for textbooks on
Jewish themes in the Russian language "in the Jewish national spirit."[22] What makes Lifshits's remarks especially
useful is precisely that he spoke in commonplaces and articulated the (widely held) view that heders and talmud-torahs
were crucial in sustaining the Jewish national spirit. At the
same time, however, he felt that he could battle with nationalist leaders while still supporting the national spirit in Jewish education. What did the term "nationalism" mean to him,
and to others like him?

First, this assertion of nationalist commitment by Russian
Jews who were not nationalists themselves, if judged on the
basis of their ideological commitments, must be seen in light
of the linguistic politics of late imperial Russia. The term *narodnost'*, best translated as "nationality" or "ethnicity," was
itself an officially designated category in Russian censuses
before the first all-Russia census in 1897, and one's classification was determined by one's native language. Nationality,
then, was a social category in a multinational empire where
non-Russians represented approximately 56% of the population by the end of the nineteenth century.[23]

The growing sense of displacement felt by Russians precipitated a particularly intense preoccupation with nationality in these years. This is evident, as Jeffrey Brooks has shown
in his study of popular literature in Russian society, in writing intended for the educated as well as the relatively unedu-
cated. In both, we encounter much anxiety about older
definitions of Russianness that were based mostly on attach-
ment to the Russian Orthodox Church and tsar. As these
banners proved less and less compelling in an increasingly
complex, multiethnic Russia, categories like the ethnically

exclusive "Russkii" were embraced over the expansive and increasingly vacuous "all-Russian" (Rossiiski). Brooks writes:

> When Georgians or Crimean Tatars were incorporated into the Russian Empire, did they become Russians who did not speak the Russian language? If not, they remained Georgians or Tatars whose loyalties were first to their own peoples, and some of whom would leave the empire at the first opportunity. There was no supra-ethnic concept of nation or empire to which diverse peoples could be attracted with a modicum of voluntarism. Yet the empire did include diverse peoples, and was expanding to include even more. The issue of what bound the empire, besides the tsar's armies, was explored implicitly in much of the popular fiction.[24]

Within this multinational Russian empire, Jews who remained optimistic about the prospect of absorption (many of the teachers at the OPE meetings fell into this category) could see themselves as part of a larger, empirewide consensus. Whatever this might mean in an ever fragmenting Russia, such integrationist Jews could continue to see themselves as part of a Jewish nationality, too.

Second, the meaning of Jewish nationalism had, of course, expanded in the late 1890s to include the non-Zionist nationalism adopted in 1901 by the Jewish Socialist Labor Bund, the major (albeit underground) socialist organization of East European Jews. Despite its illegality, it won for itself the allegiance of tens of thousands of members and many more admirers. Bundist calls for greater attention to the masses had helped inspire the OPE's decision to take heders as well as other primary schools more seriously—a reversal of a longstanding OPE preference for support of secondary and university students.[25]

Reinventing Heders

Third, the meetings examined in this chapter all occurred in the wake of a protracted battle in the OPE over the role of nationalism, the efficacy of spoken-Hebrew instruction, etc. in OPE-funded schools. By 1902, the organization had decided to fund heders and embrace (what it called) a national educational curriculum. The meaning of the term would remain in dispute, but Zionists and their allies—led by leading Russian Jewish intellectuals like Ahad Ha'am and Shimon Dubnow, who took this dispute very seriously—had triumphed. Perhaps, their opponents' unwillingness to fight nationalism openly in the meetings was, in effect, the quiet after the storm, a tacit acknowledgment that the best had to be made of a bad (hopefully, reversible) situation.[26]

None of these explanations is sufficient, however. Integrationist leaders such as Ilion, who participated in these meetings, were unlikely to be intimidated into publicly endorsing beliefs with which they disagreed. Debate in the OPE was not quashed after 1902, nor was there pressure to speak in uniformly positive terms of nationalism. What, then, accounts for these conversations?

I would suggest that it was anxiety that inspired them, an unease, sometimes expressed openly (though generally taken for granted), that Jewish youth were slipping away from things Jewish and that the disappearance of the heder would immeasurably worsen this situation. A clear articulation of the nexus between a surprisingly benign attitude to heders and fear of assimilation was made by the integrationist, anti-Zionist educator Maria Saker. She stated, at the same OPE meeting where Lifshits had made his declaration, that it was a widely held belief—one, she bemoaned, manipulated by "extreme" nationalists—that by abandoning nationalism, Jewish youth were also fleeing their own people. This was a mere canard, she insisted, little more than standard fin de siècle scare tactics and similar to the widely disseminated accusation that contemporary Russian youth were slaves to sexual depravity.[27] Yet it was widely believed at the time that a disturbing cultural slippage was taking place. Data on the enrollment of Jews in Russian schools as well as the reading habits of the Jewish young were offered as proof of how young Jews were adrift and all the more in need of old, reliable cultural moorings.

The fact that Russian schools continued to draw substantial numbers of Jews despite the quotas imposed by the government in the mid-1880s on Jewish enrollment was now seen by some leading Jewish educators (who had for years, of course, stressed the need for precisely such education for Jews) as part and parcel of an unsettling, assimilatory trend. Governmental quotas did not, on the whole, apply to girls schools, and in many towns of the Russian Pale of Settlement no fewer than half of the girls secondary school population were Jewish. Girls were excluded from Russian universities, but male externs could take qualifying examinations for university entrance (starting in 1891), and Jewish boys hoping to enter the university hired tutors for private instruction. Thousands of such tutors taught in the Pale of Settlement. Privately run schools also proliferated in Russia during these years, and a large proportion of those opened from the 1890s on were Jewish run. Moreover, quotas did not limit the enrollment of males in most state primary schools, realschulen, or commercial schools. Nor were quotas imposed with equal harshness in all educational districts: Odessa was known to be especially strict; nearby Kharkov was rather lax. All told, by 1912, 128,000 Jews were registered in Russian schools and one-quarter of this number were girls enrolled in Russian gymnasiums (classics-oriented secondary schools) or the preparatory gymnasiums.[28]

Reinventing Heders

Statistics on the reading habits of the young were also widely cited at the time. Among the many empirical studies on this topic published in these years was an article in *Ha-Shiloach* on Jewish lending-library statistics in Ukrainian Poltava. The lending library in this "typical southern Jewish town," as the article described the place, was studied in 1904–5. Subdivided were readers in the various languages (Russian, Hebrew, and Yiddish) and the various publications checked out (e.g., newspapers, school textbooks, novels, poetry, general nonfiction). In 1904–5, 35,265 items were borrowed by a total of 1,362 subscribers; 80% (28,081) were in Russian, 13% in Hebrew, and 7% in Yiddish. The majority of the items checked out were newspapers. Hebrew readers were overwhelmingly students cramming for class, not reading for pleasure. Most (70%) of the Hebrew-reading adults were laborers and artisans (i.e., the poorest and least acculturated Jews). Cultivated, middle-class Jewish readers, for whom *Ha-Shiloach* was created (Ahad Ha'am referred to them as *mevinim benonim*, or middlebrow readers, when he was the editor of the journal), constituted a mere 13%. Most middle-class readers checked out Russian books.[29]

The young were the largest group of library users: 44% were below the age of eighteen, with almost equally large numbers between the ages of eighteen and twenty-five. Of the children's books taken out, 75% were in Russian. Youth, in fact, read little Hebrew, with the exception of textbooks. Of novels read, 86% were in Russian, 9% in Yiddish, and 5% in Hebrew.[30]

Piotr Marek, veteran education activist and a leading historian of Russian Jewish education, made explicit the connection between the reading patterns of Jewish youth (as revealed in the lending patterns of libraries like the one in Poltava) and the pressing need for heder and talmud-torah reform. In the inaugural issue of *Evreiskaia shkola*, in 1904, the first journal published in the Russian language devoted exclusively to the theme of Jewish education, Marek proposed that the problem was not really the future of Jewish literacy; rather, the very "spiritual thirst" of the Jews was at stake. Proof of this, as he saw it, was the proliferation of lending libraries in nearly every townlet in the Pale of Settlement, where mostly Russian books and very few Jewish ones (he says) were sought by readers. Marek, an active Zionist, takes issue here with those sectarian Zionists ("ultranationalists") who placed their reliance on Hebrew as their primary educational tool.[31]

"What does the term 'progress' mean today?" a speaker asked rhetorically at the 1902 OPE forum in Orsha.[32] It means support for nationalist institutions, like the heder. The statement was meant to be both ironic and earnest. The minutes reveal a now forgotten dispute that evaluated the content of Jewish culture at its most basic level. A reassessment of this debate opens us to a more nuanced appreciation of cultural strategies that were, at one and the same time, self-consciously conservative yet modern, traditional yet progressive, and nationalist yet different from the nationalism of the well-known, ideologically preoccupied political parties. The strategies for maintaining a threatened Russian Jewish civilization were nothing if not eclectic.

I'm struck by the similarity between these reactions and those of historian Shimon Dubnow to his hometown Mstislavl, to which he returned a few years after his vivid denunciation of the heder quoted at the beginning of this chapter. He came back in the mid-1880s to recuperate from a long illness; like many of the Jewish intelligentsia of the time, he, too, had escaped to the city. Now he returned to his ancestral shtetl for a prolonged stay and saw Mstislavl through different eyes. In part because Dubnow had started to make a name for himself as a journalist in St. Petersburg, he no longer felt the shtetl pulling at him in quite the same way as before. In contrast to his previous desire to separate himself as decisively as possible from the place, he now sought to narrow the chasm separating him from it, and in particular, from his saintly, learned grandfather, a local spiritual leader:

> From the autumn of 1884, the following picture could be seen in the quiet provincial town: On two parallel streets grandfather and grandson sat in their book-lined studies. One cultivated the wisdom of the Talmud and the rabbis and transmitted it to his listeners; the other plunged with equal zeal into the new wisdom of the age and had his own distant, but more numerous audience. . . . Both lived like Nazarenes, obedient to strict vows, each with his own understanding of life, intellectually different, ethically identical.[33]

Crucial, in this regard, is Dubnow's assumption that his audience of Russian-language readers is the more numerous and that his grandfather's world is fast disappearing. As a result, Dubnow can afford to dwell on its virtues and he is drawn back to it with renewed commitment, or, at least, sentiment. His feelings toward Mstislavl are suddenly warm and tolerant, the product of loss and also cultural triumph, discomfort with his own triumph and alienation from a modern culture that he had sought hard to create and that, as he sees it, slips disconcertingly through one's fingers. The thick, resilient Yiddishkeit—that civilization he now embraces with affection precisely because it is, he assumes, disappearing from view—was itself born in the heders and shtetlach of

Eastern Europe. It is, as he recognizes increasingly, a thing of the past.

This is what he had earlier vigorously sought. Now, of course, it is also what he fears. His is a nostalgia born out of fear of facing a future without places like Mstislavl. These exasperating and also wonderful places were now appreciated by Dubnow for reasons quite similar to those that would later move Jews like him to embrace, however uncomfortably, the heder, too.

~ 3 ~

Remapping Odessa

I'd like to go to the real Correctionville someday. I have been living and working as a writer in the other Correctionville, the one in my mind. I am constantly tinkering with the maps of the Midwest, trying to damp the distortions as much as possible while realizing that each selected vision of the place is a map more detailed than the thing it represents.

—Michael Martone, "Correctionville, Iowa"

~

On Odessa's Richelieu Boulevard, near DeRibas (the "king" of streets in the words of Vladimir Jabotinsky), the Gessen family prepares for breakfast. The father is a grain merchant (note his good address, fine attire, and gruff, self-confident manner) in business with his father and brothers, who take commissions for the handling of grain shipped by river to Odessa and resold for export. Morning tea, a grim affair in this household, is punctuated by talk of business. Nearly all talk in this house is of business. The children escape this talk to play in the courtyard until their father gathers them in his carriage for the ride to school. Among them is Iosif Vladimirovich—born in 1866, later a leader of the Cadets, the Russian liberal party—whose memoirs provide us with this glimpse of life at the Gessen home.[1]

Young Gessen remembers riding down streets packed with grain vendors calling to his father, some stopping the carriage and talking "rapidly and insistently" in the "Jewish jargon," a language his father spoke but the children couldn't understand. Hebrew they were taught, but it never made much sense to them. There were no books at home except school texts, prayer books, and, interestingly, the pamphlets produced by a poor, "slightly mad" relative of their mother. This man was "constantly publishing, although he was poor as a church mouse. All the money he collected for the pamphlets, which he peddled himself, he used to publish new ones. What his daily bread was nobody knew and he did not seem to need any."[2] Books in this house were, in effect, consigned to madmen. We'll soon return to this theme.

By no means was this a Jewishly indifferent family—not by Odessa standards. Father was an officer of Odessa's Great Synagogue; as stipulated by Jewish ritual, the family carefully cleared away all bread items from their home prior to the Passover festival and fasted on the Day of Atonement. Still, by the time young Gessen entered university, many in this social circle had converted to Christianity. As a youth, he felt there was something tedious about Jewish ritual; in fact, the only moment of true passion he recalled was the terror that gripped his family at the prospect of economic catastrophe during the Russo-Turkish War of 1877–78, when the outlet from the Black Sea was closed and grain shipments were disrupted.[3] All that truly mattered was business. Jewish life was tepid, dry, and pointless. Gessen writes: "[E]ven in my time, all these religious traditions began to fade. The little prayer scrolls were no longer hung upon the door frames to protect the homes from ill fortune. The touching and exciting reminiscences of the thousand-year-long road of suffering became a dry conventionality, a tedious duty which one had to observe. Once it began, the assimilation of Russian culture progressed with giant strides.[4]

Books were playthings, the stuff of eccentrics or worse; life was circumscribed by the heady demands of business, especially grain. "The commercial history of Odessa *is* the history of Odessa," wrote the distinguished nineteenth-century local historian A. A. Skal'kovskii.[5] One could begin a cultural history of Jewish Odessa at the Gessen breakfast table, follow the family into the street, down Rishielevskaia, to work, (rarely) to play, to the cafe, sporadically and listlessly to synagogue.

Remapping Odessa

The materialism and the unusual opportunities available to Jews—who were the majority of leading grain exporters in Odessa, Russia's main grain-exporting port by mid-century—encouraged their mobility, ritual laxity, and acculturation. From the city's founding in 1794, Odessa's cultural institutions—a theater, later a splendid opera house—pulled at Jews, who were, at the same time, less constrained than their counterparts in most other large Jewish cities in Eastern Europe because of Odessa's distance from the centers of traditional Jewish culture. All these factors had their impact in shaping an unusual Jewish community. According to some estimates, by the 1870s, 90% of the city's Jewish-owned shops (and Jews were very important in both local wholesale and retail trade) were open on the Sabbath. All this reinforced the Yiddish saying: "Seven miles around Odessa burn the fires of Hell."[6]

A credible alternative to beginning a cultural tour of Jewish Odessa at the home of a well-situated grain merchant is to start at the workplace of a Jewish salesclerk (in 1905 the city counted about 26,000 such clerks, the vast majority of them Jews). Most were economically marginal men and women. They were compelled to dress well, which meant that many female salesclerks found themselves resorting to prostitution to supplement very meager incomes. Their hours of employment were unregulated by the state (in contrast to factory workers, for instance, who could be made to work no more than eleven and one-half hours daily); even when customers were not in the store, salesclerks were generally made to stand. The fate of such "white-handed" workers (the Russian term for white-collar, nonmanual laborers) was the inspiration for a rich part of urban folklore. Looking closely at them might help us rethink conflicting meanings of secularity, success, failure, health, and disease. They were, of course, immortalized by Isaac Babel. In Babel's short story "How It Was Done in Odessa," one of gangster Benya Krik's men accidentally kills a Jewish clerk, Yosif Mugenstein. Benya dictates the terms of an absurdly lavish funeral, where he himself delivers the oration: "Gentlemen and ladies, what did our dear Yosif get out of life? A couple of trifles. What was his occupation? He counted other people's money. . . . There are people already doomed to death, and there are people who haven't begun to live."[7]

Clearly, a cultural history of Jewish Odessa that overlooks the nexus between economics and acculturation is inadequate, as I have appreciated since this city first captured my attention several years ago. Odessa's grain Casino, the local grain center, was, in this respect at least, a Jewish "space" comparable, on its own terms, to the Vilna *shulhof*, that central courtyard in the old Jewish section of the "Jerusalem of Lithuania"; both provided a spatial framework for communal coordination, informal chat as well as economic exchange.[8]

Only the most rigid would insist that Jewish life in Odessa must be understood with the same analytic tools applied to older, more Jewishly stable, and traditional settings like Vilna, itself one of the very few positive images to emerge unsullied in the culturally fractious world of late-nineteenth-century East European Jewry. In Hasidic circles, of course, Vilna remained throughout the nineteenth century a source of misgiving as an influential anti-Hasidic stronghold. Elsewhere, though, it was roundly celebrated as an emblem of both rabbinic learning and modern Jewish scholarship, a place of study houses, streets informally named after biblical sites, and distinguished book publishers, a city where even simple Jews spoke, or so it was often claimed, a language replete with midrashic allusion. Vilna, in contrast to Odessa, was said to be a good place: appropriately (depending on one's priorities) learned, pious, politically active, communally cohesive. An indication of this standing is Samuel Joseph Fin's *Kiryah ne'emanah*, a history of Vilna published in 1860, the first history written of a Russian Jewish community and, indeed, one of the very first historical compositions written by a Russian Jew. "A prayer in every stone, a chant, a melody in every wall," as poet Moshe Kulbak would later write of Vilna. In contrast to boisterous Odessa—that unsettled city of newcomers—Vilna's Jewish population at the end of the century stood at about 60,000 (100,000 fewer Jews than in Odessa), a tightly organized, communally cohesive place, a city of 12,000 Jewish families that, or so we've been told, counted itself in families, not separate souls.[9]

I mention all this to underline the importance of beginnings: how for a historian no less than for a writer of fiction like Babel the way one begins a narrative determines something (at times a good deal) of how it is told. It should be self-evident that the story of a city can be written in numerous ways depending—again, at least in part—on where one starts. This has little necessary bearing on accuracy. Sources must be interpreted accurately, of course, but the historian may choose which to use, and such choices have a decisive impact on the texture and trajectory of the resulting narrative. Choosing one set of sources or narrative strategy over another depends on calculations of historical priority, transparency, and significance. All these are—in large and small ways—influenced by individual inclinations that the historian cannot always be aware of.

Stuart Hampshire puts these rather self-evident truisms well: "The significance of a writer, whether poet or philosopher or historian, and that which makes him worthy of study now, commonly does not reside principally in the conscious intention behind his work, but rather in the precise nature, as we can now see it, of the conflicts and the imaginative inconsistencies in his work."[10]

In this vein, I interrogate my abiding fascination with Odessa. I construct this essay around texts which helped me determine how to start the telling of its story. My relationship with these texts (mostly maskilic, or Jewish Enlightenment in nature) has long been complex, usually adversarial, as I have understood it, in that I found them useful for their social and cultural evidence but nearly always problematic in their assumptions about the city and (as most of them asserted) its cultural deficiencies.

To understand what I mean (my predicament, at least in this respect, can be seen as somewhat typical of writers of Russian Jewish history until the opening of archival material in the former USSR in the last few years), remember that those of us who write about the Russian Jewish past have for much of this century been dependent mostly on printed sources located almost entirely in the West. Archival research in the Soviet Union was closed to Judaica scholars, and the bulk of available material (the sort of material on which my own history of Odessa Jewry was built) is almost exclusively in the form of newspapers and journals, Jewish and non-Jewish. Fortunately, there was a vast periodical press in imperial Russia, with Jewish newspapers in a range of languages: Russian, Hebrew, and Yiddish. Still, articles in this press were often skewed in rather predictable ways and, as printed sources, were sometimes heavily censored (or self-censored), and nearly all were produced by intellectuals of one sort or another.

Imagine a history of Los Angeles without access to local archives and guided mainly by the dark ruminations on L.A. of Bertolt Brecht or Nathaniel West. I exaggerate, but not wildly. Russian Jewish intellectuals (and so-called half-intellectuals) viewed Odessa in much the way that twentieth-century intellectuals tend to see Los Angeles: vapid, flamboyant, mercenary, all-too-enticing. Exceptions are rare, and self-conscious of how they break the mold. Isaac Babel is one; Vladimir Jabotinsky (who wrote the unusual celebration of Jewish businessmen in Odessa) is another. In any event, the primary sources on Odessa Jewry until the recent opening of Russian and Ukrainian archives were the numerous newspaper and journal articles by writers who, on the whole, loathed, or at least patronized, the city.[11]

The dean of Russian Jewish historiography, Shimon Dubnow, called Odessa "the least historical of all cities," and he lived there for the most fertile years of his scholarly and journalistic life, between 1890 and 1903. This city, insisted Dubnow, essentially had no history; it was crass, commercial, brash, and irrelevant.[12] Such judgments were, I insisted when I wrote my first book, misleading historically. If it was commerce that had a decisive impact on local culture—with the demands of commerce openly fueling the building of the famed Odessa opera house, schools, and local museums—this should be analyzed, not excoriated.

I revisit here two memoirs and one Hebrew novel, all of which hold the city accountable for failing in one way or another to live up to hegemonic, abstract standards set mainly by the urban exemplar of Vilna: a cerebral, learned place valued by rabbinic scholar and so-called enlightened Jew alike. What I find surprising in rereading these sources after several years is how sympathetic I find them, the extent to which I concur (and probably always concurred) with at least some of their more important assumptions about Odessa. These assumptions are, I understand, rigid, probably excessively so. They assume a preference for a bookish, literate culture and view boisterous, materialistic Odessa from the margins, from the vantage point of intellectuals who, when thinking about the place, are rendered glum, envious, and scandalized, outside in the cold. This is, I now realize, uncannily similar to my own thinking about the place. And, ironically, it is for this reason that I have long remained fixated on the city as a cultural signpost in contemporary Jewish life.

First, let us examine a sketch written by Elhonon Levinsky, an Odessa Hebraist of note, a member of the entourage of the Jewish nationalist cultural leader Ahad Ha'am. In an 1896 essay called "City of Life," he reflects on what might be called the wages of cultural space in Jewish Odessa. He begins by telling how he finds himself passing, sometimes with sadness, a building on Langeron Street, a bustling cafe that a few years earlier had been a reading room. Here, for a mere five kopecks, a reader could sit all day with the world's best literature. The room was nearly always empty. A newcomer to Odessa, he queried its owner as to why, in a city full of "men of enlightenment and readers of books," it didn't attract more readers, and the proprietor answered with what now seemed to Levinsky an uncanny prescience. He said that if he opened a cafe, it would be packed.Odessa Jews enjoy, as he put it, boisterous activity, rich food, and harsh coffees, never books. Even when a couple of poor Jews meet on the street, the information they exchange is about the current price of the ruble. Hence, the city's cultural institutions, impressive from afar, languish from neglect. Donations from the local rich are erratic and meager.[13]

Still musing on the now-thriving cafe, Levinsky remarks how the same remoteness from learning and high culture leaves its stamp on local Jewish life. Judaism here is a spectator sport, a passive exercise in curiosity, quaint, even kitsch. This is what he describes when he brings us to a city park in the early evening with its minstrels and other delights. Here is a Jewish minstrel named Davidov singing ditties he calls "the songs of the Jews," telling stories from the lives of the Jews, and dancing Jewish dances. Onstage surrounded by laughing patrons, Davidov dons a prayer shawl and phylacteries, drawing into the act Gentiles as well as Jews with the assurance that they too, if they wish, can be good, kosher Jews just like him. The crowd loves him, Jews and non-Jews alike crying for more, begging him to tell more stories from the Jewish past. The Jews of Odessa, Levinsky writes, are the first to pay good money for the sheer pleasure (as he puts it) of having "dirty water" tossed in their faces. Predictably, Levinsky, a native of Lithuania, compares these odd, troubling features of life to conditions back home and, in comparison, the Black Sea port comes out looking awful.[14]

My second text is an appraisal of Mendele Mocher Seforim in turn-of-the-century Odessa. By then Mendele had achieved, as is well known, an extraordinary standing among East European Jewry as its greatest writer of Hebrew, as well as Yiddish, prose. The best proof of this stature and popularity is his 1909 lecture tour throughout Eastern Europe, the grandest tour of a Jewish writer of the time. Even the sardonic David Frischman (probably the most dour Jewish literary critic of the time in the Russian empire) observed that no Jewish writer had ever encountered such a reception: "The 'triumphal tour' went from Vilna to Bialystok, from Bialystok to Warsaw, from Warsaw to Lodz. No other writer —Jew or Gentile—has ever been accorded such an honor. It was the journey of a duke. Thousands of people waited at each train station, thousands of people jostled and pushed each other to approach him, happy if they managed to shake his hand or even just catch a glimpse of his face."[15]

Remapping Odessa

Presumably Odessa, where Mendele had lived since 1880 as director of the local, educationally innovative talmud-torah, treated him similarly. Imagine the surprise of writer Yitshak Dov Berkowitz, son-in-law of Sholem Aleichem, when, as a newcomer to Odessa, he finds Mendele wandering the city streets for hours without being recognized, gathering much of the material for his fiction, spying on conversations. Mendele could do this with efficiency because, though lionized elsewhere, he walked Odessa's streets relatively unnoticed. Perhaps Berkowitz exaggerates, but his sense of Mendele's predicament (which, as it happens, is how Mendele, too, saw the situation) remains revealing. Berkowitz writes: "Mendele would go and walk around in Odessa, and there were very few of the local population who knew that he was the old, honored man. And if there was someone who happened to remark that this was Mendele, the news would seem entirely strange: Mendele? Who is this Mendele? A Hasidic rebbe? A good, pious Jew? A wonder-worker? What is this sort of person doing in Odessa?" [16]

I'll return to what I think this means in a moment. My final example is, among other things, further testimony to how firmly Vilna had imposed itself on the Jewish cultural imagination, defining in the process what responsible, credible cultural change was, and what it wasn't. I refer to Reuven Braudes's 1888 novel *Shete ha-ketsavot* (The two extremes), described by literary historian Joseph Klausner as the first significant novel in the Hebrew language.[17] Here we find a series of interlinked tales, at whose core is the story of a very wealthy, young Hasid who comes to Odessa and, without so much as reading a line of a serious book (he does dip into a few poems and stories of romance), is transformed. True, he manages to teach himself to read music to play a flute, but this is his closest brush with high culture. Braudes intends for us to see Hasid Yaakov Hetzron's transformation as a tale of cultural change gone wrong; indeed, at the novel's end he is saved, rendered suitably modern, by a Vilna Jew who rescues him from the rudderless change characteristic of Odessa, devoid of intellectual underpinnings.

Of the very few unequivocal heroes in this book—Jews of moderate appetite with healthy respect for modernity as well as tradition—nearly all come from Vilna. They attempt to influence wayward souls, to translate maskilic Vilna's chief message: careful, cerebral, muted reform and, above all, the primacy of ideas.

We first meet Hasidic protagonist Yaakov Hetzron a week after his arrival in Odessa, sitting in Alexandrovskii Park overlooking the sea, gazing out at the water and contemplating its power and mystery: "A precious sight, a very lovely sight. Here, he saw beauty face to face; here splendor and order met; loveliness and regimen joined together. . . . It brought his soul down to the very depths and made his heart throb. The beauty of the city was beyond estimation." [18] In what is a rather rambling novel, Yaakov doesn't really move much beyond this point. True, he leaves the seaside perch, and we follow him into middle-class drawing rooms and, with particular frequency, to the home of the merchant Achitov, whose daughter Liza wins his heart. Emotionally, though, Yaakov is fixed throughout the novel at much the same point we first encounter him. He is, in fact, a remarkably passive fellow who is led in tow place after place by the novel's true villain, his attorney Yurav (a linguistic play, I think, on the biblical sinner Jeroboam, the son of Nevat). Yurav takes him to cabarets and bars, as well as to middle-class salons, and it is in these places—not in the time-honored,

canonized maskilic routine that begins cultural moderni-
zation with a reading of Moses Mendelssohn, Spinoza, or
Moshe Leib Lilienblum—it is in such rooms and not in libraries that Yaakov is made over: "His faith died a painless
death, without any battle, without anguish of heart and
soul."[19]

Yaakov is taken early in the novel to the concert hall, but
we aren't told what he hears; the joy is in sitting in a marvelous room with *sarim ve-sarot* (dignitaries, male and female), close to his beloved Liza.[20] He spends his waking
hours wandering streets and parks in search of Liza; the characters in the novel, the males especially, rarely seem to sleep
a full night, the least stressful encounter triggering bouts
of sleeplessness. Liza herself is a rather unexceptional soul:
manipulative, fickle, without, it seems, much affection for
Yaakov. She comes alive mostly in Yaakov's fervid, sleep-
deprived mind. Much here is abstraction, especially love:
"Love. Love for a girl! A new word and a new feeling for
Yaakov Hetzron. A feeling he had never known before today,
nor had he ever heard the word until today."[21] He learns
about love from books, and the only books he reads during
his stay in Odessa are romances. In a splendid subversion of
a Jewish Enlightenment motif, it is venal Yurav who plies
Yaakov with literature—cheap, dime-store novels that corrupt his soul.

Braudes, an innovative novelist, is aware of what he is doing when he has the manipulative cad Yurav lead Yaakov to
the only books he reads in Odessa. This bout of reading follows in the wake of a motivational speech of Yurav's in which
he insists (in mock-maskilic fashion) that his Hasidic friend
must broaden his horizons with literature. It is tawdry books
that reshape his vocabulary and behavior as an alternative

Shulchan Aruch, of sorts, setting down specifications for behavior and speech alike.

There are still worse problems in paradise: Yaakov, who has posed as a childless widower, is actually a married man with children back home in his native townlet Sukkoth. Eventually he is found out. Yurav presses him to divorce his wife and marry Liza, whose father (a client of Yurav's threatened with bankruptcy) would be saved by a rich son-in-law. This is why Yurav has been plying the Hasid with romance literature: to excite Yaakov with the promise of love so that he throws his family overboard for Liza.

The plot thickens further when Liza's brother, exhausted by the frivolities of life in Odessa, and especially his empty, self-seeking wife, arranges to have himself sent on business to Sukkoth. There he is moved by the dignity of Jewish ritual practice (of which he knows precious little, it seems), and he is overwhelmed by the—quite literally—unvarnished beauty of Sukkoth's women. In contrast to Yaakov's introduction at the seashore, we first meet Shlomo in Sukkoth at the Sabbath table. Here, again, a telling feature of this text is its examination of the differences in Jewish "space" in big city and townlet, as reflected in each journey's beginning.

Shlomo promptly falls in love with a commendable young woman in Sukkoth, Yaakov's sister-in-law Shifra. Shlomo encounters—and, of course, is appalled by—the fanaticism of the place, but he dallies, unwilling to take up again his old life in Odessa. Yaakov remains in Odessa, where eventually he learns that the city's glitter hides an ugly, rapacious side. In the end, a decorously enlightened Vilna Jew, a long-lost grandfather, sets everyone on course: he even teaches Yaakov's Hasidic wife proper grooming techniques, whereupon she dazzles her ever-impressionable husband when she sweeps into town.

Remapping Odessa

This is, as the title warns us, a study in extremes: Odessa and Sukkoth; Liza's brother Shlomo and the erstwhile Hasid Yaakov; Liza and the modest, literate Shifra. In the midst of this chaos, long-lost relatives surface to reclaim progeny, errant husbands and wives are reconciled, Yaakov comes to see Odessa as the frivolous place we always knew it to be, and the novel ends with a promise of reconciliation between the jagged sides of Jewish life.

Odessa here is, by and large, a place that tears people apart: it turns monsters like Yurav loose to corrupt the weak and impressionable. It bewitches Yaakov into thinking he has found happiness; it promises easy pleasure and riches; it persuades the naive and incredulous that its physical beauty represents something profound. In Sukkoth, a benighted place, there is still the Sabbath; in Odessa, there are cheap thrills, momentary pleasures, sensuous, startling glimpses of sea or urban paradise that yield little beyond their surfaces.

When many years ago I first read *Shete ha-ketsuvot*, it helped shape my impression that to write about this city required different analytic tools than might be necessary for other East European Jewish communities. Thus one would avoid an exaggerated reliance on the influence of books, intellectuals, and self-conscious cultural production. I remain convinced that this is true. A history of Odessa with intellectuals at the center—in other words, told in terms of an intimate reciprocity between intellectual production and an eager Jewish milieu of the sort that, we are told, existed in Vilna—would distort local cultural history and the role intellectuals played. The place of Jewish intellectuals in the shaping of local cultural life was marginal; this marginality must be seen as a part of the city's Jewish story.

Consequently, or so I then assumed, I used maskilic, or Enlightenment, sources in order to unsettle their assumptions about the city and what it represented in modern Jewish life. The story of the intellectuals themselves was an epiphenomenon in a historical analysis whose trajectory began elsewhere: in the grain Casino, so to speak, rather than in the study. This is how I understood until recently the intention of my work: an attempt to tease out of mostly maskilic texts what could be learned about the city's economic and social life, its high, as well as its popular, culture.

It was three years ago in the State Archives in Odessa, housed in what was until the 1920s the prestigious Brodskaia Synagogue (whose history I was the first to reconstruct in my book), that I recognized, rather vaguely initially, that I had not been altogether frank with myself about what most interested me about this city. I sat surrounded by far more archival material on Odessa Jews than could be absorbed in ten lifetimes: banking records of its wealthiest Jews, transcripts of its Jewish organizational meetings, commercial records dating back to the immigration of several hundred Jewish merchants from Galicia in the 1820s, who had a considerable commercial, as well as cultural, impact on local Jewish life, police reports describing the daily routine (not surprisingly, rather mundane) of physician and proto-Zionist leader Leon Pinsker.

It was now that I realized, handling material suddenly and easily accessible to me, that much of what was in my possession did not provide me with the sort of knowledge that had sustained my interest in the city over the years. Here, again we return to matters of origin: how a story is shaped by the way it begins. It now became clear to me that my fascination with Odessa remained focused still, oddly enough, on the same intellectuals whose shavings of cultural reality, whose artifacts, I had reviewed in the past mostly for reasons of utility—or so I thought.

Remapping Odessa

I had relied primarily on their sources because, I assumed, so little else was available on which to base an assessment of life in this city. It now became clear, once the Russian archival material that I had sought for years was made readily accessible, that what intrigued me most about this city was the relationship that intellectuals had with it. For years this awkward, unsettling relationship had provided me, as I now see it, with a metaphor for something still larger, for the often tenuous relationship in contemporary life between self-conscious producers of ideas and the larger community of Jews. Odessa was for me, above all, a splendid prism through which to study a poignant, and culturally crucial, relationship in modern Jewish life, and the purpose for which I might now use newly available archival material on the city would probably be to explicate much the same historical problems in terms, say, of the relationship between female intellectuals and the larger Jewish sphere. Otherwise, the city—beautiful, though it was—held little compelling fascination for me.

In other words, I had long believed that my goal as a historian, difficult as this was without access to archives, was to tell the story of Odessa Jews from its center: from the vantage point of its merchants, its business community, its sturdy, well-funded institutions, its confident, acculturated Jews. But I now see that what most intrigued me all along was life at its margins: the city as seen through the eyes of its maskilic newcomers, young men from the provinces, to recycle Lionel Trilling's still-suggestive phrase (with newly accessible archives providing, I suspect, much about their female counterparts), who come to town with grand expectations and who are disappointed in the worst of ways. They are disappointed not by fanatics (a rather tepid, unpowerful lot here), whose familiar attentions would, in any event, have been flattering.

79

Remapping Odessa

Rather, our maskilim, our heroes inspired by Jewish Enlightenment aspirations, encounter the terrible, numbing sensation of being rendered irrelevant with few interested readers, a communal establishment neither shocked nor, for that matter, much interested, and (perhaps this was most hurtful) modern, progressive youth who look right past them. Here, in a place that was the most "modern" in Russian Jewry, or so they had come to believe, maskilic intellectuals found that they had within the span of a short train ride of a day or two passed from small-town notoriety to irrelevance. Back home, they were the worst of transgressors. Now, in a place where there were publishers, jobs, schools, even freedom from hecklers—here there was little apparent need for them.

The stuff of tragedy, a grim signpost in contemporary Jewish life: the *tref posul,* that forbidden book so dangerous and enticing elsewhere, no longer threatens here. This is because scholars, whether traditional or modern, no longer intimidate. Isn't there something unsettling in this, if only in its familiarity?

Odessa Jewry's story, as I now recognize I've been inclined to tell it, begins neither at the commercial exchange nor the port, not even in the city itself, but on the train. I begin with a passenger, a young maskil, an erudite lapsed rabbinic scholar or Hasid, a peripatetic youth from Lithuania or the Ukraine. The Hebrew writer Yaakov Fichman tells of his own journey: "I stood nearly the entire night beside an open train carriage window breathing the fragrance of the dark, vast southern steppe."[22] He comes from a primitive place with few good books, some camaraderie, much darkness. He is barely able to contain himself because he is on his way to Odessa.

The train trip is a crucial part of his spiritual journey, as recalled in memoirs written years later. It is almost always the longest distance he has traveled; it offers his first sense of the world's immensity, of his life as an unfolding adventure, of a real distance from the battlefield of his adolescence. He will soon see the Black Sea. Still more exciting, he will be near (or so he hopes) the "wise men of Odessa"—the so-called *hakhmei Odessa*—those arbiters of good taste, culture, and politics. He imagines himself sitting at the poet Bialik's table, in publicist Ahad Ha'am's sitting room, holding in his hands the galleys of his own articles or poetry, praised by giants. He feels joy, fear, ambition, overpowering expectation: he steps off the train into the night air smelling of greenery.[23]

It is young Jewishly preoccupied *intelligenty*, like Fichman, hungry to escape the world of their fathers and mothers (and no less eager for an embrace)—intellectuals who rush off to Odessa from their parental homes as angry rebels and, once there, readily adopt Mendele as their "grandfather" and Sholem Aleichem (or, for that matter, Ahad Ha'am) as their "father"—such ambivalent, ambiguous modernists have been for many years my main interest. Odessa fascinates me as a backdrop to these lives, as a setting for an extraordinary and ironic encounter. Here they come fleeing the shackles of small-town Jewish life with a sense of urgency to do their part in creating a new understanding of Judaism in modernity. They produce much of their best work here in a place that inspires and horrifies them.

In the late 1880s and early 1890s, an unusually talented pool of "transitional" or maskilic intellectuals, writers mostly of Hebrew or Yiddish eager to leave their mark on Jewish life, arrive in Odessa. This group has a small inner circle of no more than twenty young men (the one woman who belongs, Maria Saker, is typically little known), and these intellectuals quickly set themselves apart from those they designate as their inferiors and whom they manage, quite effectively, to write out of history.[24]

Later, when they and their literary heirs reconstructed the Russian Jewish past—once they resettled in post–World War I Berlin, Tel Aviv, and elsewhere—they recalled Mendele and his circle as situated at the center of local Jewish cultural life. Beginning in the 1920s, once the collected works of Mendele and other writers in this literary stable were codified, it was this collective memory of what had transpired in Odessa (along, ironically, with sweeping denunciations of the city) that was imposed on twentieth-century Jewry, and in the absence of a culturally active Russian Jewry in the Soviet Union, these images would remain on the whole uncontested.

When we look at this circle in Odessa at their prime, however, we find intellectual pioneers with the saddest of voices. Dubnow, a shrewd observer, saw this when he reviewed in a well-known article an early venture of this group, the journal *Kaveret* of the late 1880s. In *Kaveret* and elsewhere, this circle communicated the sense that as crucial as their tasks were (they saw themselves as doing little less than reconstructing a now threatened Jewish civilization), they would most probably fail. The reasons for their pessimism had little to do with antisemitism, per se. Countervailing cultural forces in the West as well as in Russia were, simply, too powerful, the pull of the larger world too strong. This response is more than merely idiosyncratic: it was not merely that Bialik resisted the crown of the national poet (which, of course, he assiduously courted as well), that Ahad Ha'am's depressions got the better of him, or that Mendele resented all political camps and designations and poked fun at them all. Rather, their pessimism was something of a cultural trademark, a defining feature of the time and place and their response to them.

Their ideologies, among the most influential in twentieth-century Jewish life, were conceived against this backdrop of abiding loss. Like Levinsky, who admits he cannot help but return to the site of that once empty private lending library and look in at the now garrulous crowd inside (a scene, as he describes it, of loneliness and embarrassment), I too find the marginality of Odessa's intellectuals a cruel source of fascination. In a place that they had fully expected to conquer, they lived as something of a colony, spying on street-corner performers, on clowns whose impact on local Jewry was, as they understood it, more decisive than theirs because these performers had somehow managed to transmute Jewish culture into something both vague and, surprisingly, facile.

Lonely now for the first time in their lives, or so they assert often (Moshe Leib Lilienblum's memoirs, *Hatot Neurim*, provide one of Hebrew literature's best portraits of big-city ennui in their depiction of his first years in Odessa), these intellectuals evoke a longing of their own for the self-contained Jewish towns where they were once shunned, persecuted, and also important. The sadness in their writings is inspired by the view of what they left behind from the perspective of their new, painfully marginal urban perch. Not that they can forget altogether the bite of small-town fanaticism. Still, its veneration for those who write and its respect for those who read are all the more apparent to them now; they sense it might well prove impossible in Odessa to construct a credible modernized version of Judaism that could be sturdy enough to sustain the burden. Ahad Ha'am gave the impression publicly of an austere, almost eerie self-confidence. Yet take a look at one of his first pieces, written in the volume *Kaveret* before his famous essay "Lo zeh ha-derekh" (This is not the way). This semiautobiographical piece "Ketavim balim" (A tattered manuscript) is an elegy:

> But what am I now? A maskil? I cannot say that with certainty. Still now, in the moments before the end of the Sabbath, between the time that the sun sets and one begins lighting candles once again, I love to sit in a corner in the dark and examine the range of my feelings. In such moments, I feel my soul rising heavenward, as if my spiritual elation has emerged from within me to the sound of heavenly voices, and I recall various memories of my youth, memories that make me laugh, pleasant recollections—recollections that please me very much. . . . Sometimes my lips will open as if by themselves, and I find myself chanting some well-known melody in a hushed voice. . . . During those long winter evenings, at times when I'm sitting in the company of enlightened men and women, sitting at a table with *tref* food and cards, and my heart is glad and my face bright, suddenly then—I don't know how this happens—suddenly before me is a very old table with broken legs, full of tattered books [*sefarim balim*], torn and dusty books of genuine value, and I'm sitting alone in their midst, reading them by the light of a dim candle, opening up one and closing another, not even bothering to look at their tiny print . . . and the whole world is like the Garden of Eden.[25]

The table is broken; the books are dusty, tattered; his joy in reading them is incomparable. He imagines the scene with fierce longing because there is, of course, now an unbridgeable distance between him and that world, which he can never reenter. Nor, for that matter, would he wish to. Still, the vacuous scene in which he now finds himself (with its drink, cards, a hint of promiscuity) is contrasted with the *beis medresh*, this idyll. Past and also future are reconfigured; the distance between books sacred and profane is collapsed. Having seen what Odessa has wrought, he imagines a conservative utopia: a return to a time when joy was in study, when authority was in the hands of those who best read texts, when the boundaries of what was and wasn't Jewish were—or, at least appeared to be—self-evident.

"Just wait until now becomes then. You'll see how happy we were," writes Susan Sontag.[26] Many of the *hakhmei Odessa* ("wise men" like Dizengoff, Ahad Ha'am, Ravnitsky) would later seek to impose much the same vision and create from scratch in the sand dunes near ancient Jaffa a city inspired both by what Odessa was and, more important, by what it was not: a seaside utopia, a homogeneously Jewish but (as they saw it) liberal kingdom with its emblem of literacy, its gymnasium, at the center of the town. This elite school was at the town's topographical—and ideological—center as the earliest maps show; Ahad Ha'am, the moral philosopher of a reconstructed bourgeois, secular Jewishness, was placed in a house around the corner from the school in what was to be a world of comfortable burghers and literate, urban Jews. This Mediterranean Hampstead Garden suburb was, of course, quickly transformed in the mid-1920s by tens of thousands of Jews, mostly small shopkeepers and artisans from Poland, who built a nervous, vibrant town that without premeditation shunted aside the plans of its intellectual founders. The city grew; the gymnasium, stuck at one of its now remote corners, was leveled; a Hebrew-speaking culture of a different sort emerged.

"Forget for a while that you've got spectacles on your nose and autumn in your soul. Stop raising hell at your desk and stammering in public," instructs Isaac Babel's Aryeh Leib, sitting on the Odessa cemetery wall telling of the life of that noble savage Benya Krik.[27] Those unable to follow this impossible dictum (ironic fare that Babel himself was far from sure ought to be followed) stare at the town and its people with awe, with exasperation, and with an awareness of that chasm that is, in many respects, their Muse.

~ 4 ~

On the Holocaust
in the Writing of
the East European
Jewish Past

Before that—the dreadful field, sown with mangled men, in-
human cruelty, unbelievable wounds, fractured skulls, naked
young bodies gleaming white in the sun, jettisoned note-
books, leaflets, soldiers' books, Bibles, bodies amidst the
wheat.

—Isaac Babel, *1920 Diary*

~

This chapter is inspired by a new, unsettling acquaintance with a region that Jewish historians have studied for too long from afar.[1] This new familiarity has made me all the more attentive to critical literature about the possibility of historical coherence and rationality in the shadow of a catastrophe that stretches the limits of representational categories of knowledge.

The London-based historical geographer David Lowenthal raises especially intriguing, unnerving questions that might be usefully pondered by historians of East European Jews. Addressing those who claim they are capable of reconstructing the past without being encumbered by what has transpired more recently, he reminds us that "the past as reconstructed is always more coherent than when it happened. We have to interpret the ongoing present as we live through it, whereas we stand outside the past to view its more finished forms, including its now known consequences for what was then the unknown future."[2]

Such insights (self-evident, it now seems, but also rather subversive) only began to make sense once I had traveled back and forth to Russia and Poland in the last few years; these experiences made me begin to rethink the interrelationship between newly accessible archival material and experiential knowledge. New archival material happily provides us with the prospect of a more expansive basis from which to reconstruct Jewish history. But these are not the only new sources open to us as historians of East European Jewry. The interplay between an array of new inspirations—textual, physical, and experiential—is at the core of this chapter.

No lesson has been driven home with quite the same force in Russian Jewish historiography as the need for distance and dispassion. This is a central theme already in the first historiographical essays on the subject: the Russian- and Hebrew-language statements written by Shimon Dubnow, published in 1891 and 1892. These essays are generally credited, with good reason, with having launched systematic writing on the subject.[3]

At the heart of these pioneering articles is a preoccupation with the pitfalls of empathy in work readily disfigured by passion. It is astonishing, in fact, to see how early this theme rises to the top of the Russian Jewish historiographical agenda. In short, a distorted and severely constrained collective memory is pitted from the outset against a modulated and contextual scholarship written to unsettle these very popular assumptions.

Here is Dubnow, in 1892, summing up how pitifully little Russian Jews appear to know about their past: a startlingly brief list that includes no more than the one published Hebrew account of the seventeenth-century Chmielnitski massacres and a random grab bag of historical moments, a name of a great early modern rabbi, terms like the "Council of the Four Lands" or "Cossacks." He places vast importance on a historical consciousness among Jews.

> Only in our midst, among the Jews of Poland and Russia, has there been kindled no desire to uncover the secrets of our past, to know what we were, how we came to our present

circumstances and how our forefathers lived during the eight
hundred years beginning with the start of Jewish life in
Poland. There are times when I suspect in my heart that we
altogether lack historical feeling. As if we were . . . like gypsies
whose lives are entirely in the present and who have neither
a future nor a past. And the few, select ones so inclined to
know the shape of the past actually recognize merely frag-
ments of things and scattered incidents.[4]

In these historiographical essays, we find the argument for
a stark disjuncture between the (laudatory and empirical)
goals of history and the imperfections of memory. However,
once we look beyond these bald assertions, there is much
here that is far more interesting in that it undermines Dubnow's otherwise facile distinctions between the various ways
of knowing about the past. Especially since Dubnow seeks
to make historical consciousness the basis for a reconstructed Jewish identity, the essays (in particular, the Hebrew-
language version) recognize that there is a tension between
history's goals of analytic rigor and existential utility. These
pieces may be revisited usefully today as an intriguing, anxious road map for the Jewish historian: a portrait of the
uneasy relationship between detachment and engagement,
metahistory and social history, historical knowledge as a
substitute for religious faith and as a transparent, unmediated source of truth about the world.

Indeed, immediately after Dubnow sets down the claims
for historical empiricism, he declaims, in the unmistakable
voice of a *maggid*, or preacher, that the writing of history will,
as he puts it, breathe new life into the old bones of the Jewish
people: It is time, he insists, to awaken the slumbering, to
gather together the scattered memorials of the nation's past.
"My purpose in life has been made clear," the young man
writes in a diary entry for, significantly, New Year's Day 1892.

On the Holocaust

"I have become a 'missionary of history.'"[5] The essays themselves challenge his own deeply felt, sincere positivist convictions in their foregrounding of existential goals and in their unabashed use of history as a balm for the Jewish people. From its moment of origin, Russian Jewish historiography is torn from within by tensions that remain surprisingly relevant to the present day.

Dubnow's searing declamations have been seen as an embarrassing, if understandable, shortcoming for a man of integrity and erudition caught in the dark years of late imperial Russia. Rather than viewing these as testimony to his lapses from sobriety, it may be more useful to consider the two central features of Dubnow's essays—their simultaneous insistence on detachment and their evident, pronounced fierce engagement with the subject matter and, in particular, with the people who are its subject and the author's overriding passion—as two sides of the same coin.

In this respect, I find especially intriguing the essays' link between the collation of archival sources, the demands for a sober historiography, and its powerful authorization of history as an answer to the needs of the folk. Dubnow admits that the Hebrew version of the essay was produced for the express purpose of inspiring yeshiva students, rabbis, and others to ferret through the storage rooms of synagogues and study houses for discarded, historically important material. It was an inspirational document directed at the Jewish people's young rabbinic elite and it readily adopted their own seductive, resonant discourse.

Primary material, as he reports in his autobiography, soon started pouring into his house (he had given it, for lack of any other obvious location, as the address where the sources should be sent), and he describes how he cleared out a drawer in his desk for the first bits and pieces of material and thus established the first archive for Russian Jewish history.[6] The simple act is touching and it should remind us of the mundane, domestic origins of what it is that Jewish historians do.

The systematic study of Russian Jewish history was launched, then, by a young, still fairly obscure journalist living precariously on a rather grim street around the corner from the kosher butchers' synagogue of Odessa (later the building was a local KGB listening station) who established the field's first coherent archive by urging yeshiva students to supply him with whatever scraps they could locate. From the beginning this was a historiography that was intimately invested in the politics and passions of the folk and that, as a result, insisted all the more emphatically on its scientific credentials and dispassion.

Our preoccupation, as historians, with the ferocity of immigrant memory is not unreasonable. Indeed, books tarnished with the sin of being "presentist"—that is, of looking at the past with too fixed a view of the present or, at least, of events outside the immediate purview of the historical actors they examine—have long, and with justification, been our most obvious, vivid foils. Books that imagined a pre-Holocaust Jewish life as teetering on the "edge of destruction" were those that helped define as readily as anything else the boundaries of acceptable historical discourse. Few preoccupations have loomed quite so large in East European historiography's sense of its own parameters: a more or less consensual designation of what falls on either side of good or bad scholarly discourse. In other words, a self-consciously modulated and contextual scholarship written, in part, to unsettle popular accounts was promoted. Anxiety defined the popular versions of this past. For the other, however, anxieties of all sorts were played down excessively in an attempt to set the record straight by redressing the balance.[7]

If we were to begin to capture the folk's own sense of the content of tsarist life, we cannot overlook the fact that millions, quite literally, spoke at the turn of the twentieth century with their feet. The Zionists affirmed the need to abandon Russia in the most emphatic, ideological terms (they saw the pogrom years 1881 and 1903 as definitive turning points in Jewish history, for example), but across the Jewish cultural and political spectrum there existed a consensus that Russia was fundamentally a horrible place. "Darkest Russia" was, appropriately, the name of the most consistently lacerating periodical about life under the tsars published in a Western language prior to World War I, and it was financed (albeit secretly) by London's Jewish elite. By 1905, if any issue united downtown and uptown, Russell Square and East End, the Jews of Germany, England, and the United States, it was the suffering of the Jews of Eastern Europe.[8]

The historical literature on the topic was rather sparse after the vigorous, productive decades leading up to World War I until the rebirth of interest in the 1960s and 1970s in the United States, Israel, and Europe. Historical literature produced in the 1920s in the Soviet Union on the subject was, on the whole, heavily larded with ideological constraints. The Yiddish language, in which much of Soviet scholarship was written, further marginalized it among historians in this century. Much of the work produced on East European Jewish history in interwar Poland concentrated on early modern history, and it, too, was cut short by the war. Even before, university restrictions on the appointment and training of Jewish historians meant that mostly amateurs of varying levels of sophistication and background mined the area. Beginning in the 1930s, few scholars in the Soviet Union risked working openly on the history of the Jews, although literary and linguistic work appeared with somewhat greater frequency.[9]

In the absence of fresh historical work, in the wake of fierce, definitive immigrant memories about what life back there was like, and in the aftermath of the Shoah, pervasive premonitions of horror regarding Eastern Europe were conflated and granted a grim prescience: Nazi horrors and tsarist pogroms meshed in the often sparse, repetitive narratives that Jews tended to tell about this vast, complex region. The distance between life in Vilna and death in Treblinka tended to narrow in such accounts, as if these were mere differences in detail, not substance. Even the revival of the term "shtetl" in the 1950s and 1960s as a good thing—as a place of happily unencumbered identity and family peacefulness—did little to unsettle this portrait, especially since shtetlach were celebrated as tenuous, fragile entities, all the more precious because they were surrounded by deadly forces. Here, too, the primary message was one of misery and despair, a sliver of beauty in a domain ruled by Cossacks.

Eastern Europe was, in turn, emptied, drained of color, texture, and complexity. What remained—aside from often the most random recollections of humiliation—was little more than the name of a town, a province, perhaps a river. "'And just where, exactly, was this place, this house . . . ?'" asks Simon Schama of his mother, as he writes in his recent book, *Landscape and Memory.* "I pressed my mother while we sat eating salad in a West End hotel. For the first time in my life I badly needed to know. 'Kowno guberniia, outside Kowno, that's all we ever knew.' She shrugged her shoulders and went back to her lettuce." [10]

Whether strained, emotional terrain or a hopelessly, perhaps evasively uncertain one—such attitudes of the Jewish

On the Holocaust

folk were often close to the surface in what we did as historians. They provided dark, stark, convenient foils, misperceptions which were both deeply unsettling and also strangely inspiring. I think of this as not wholly dissimilar to how the outpouring of mostly negative Jewish reactions to *Goodbye, Columbus* so unsettled—and also inspired—Philip Roth, providing him with a heightened, sharpened measure of his task and with a fictional theme for much of the rest of his career.[11] For us, too, our own lives and work are conducted against a strained, overwrought backdrop which helped to prod us on. We were, in this regard at least, ersatz maskilim wrestling with obdurate forces. Our task was to implode collective memory, to juxtapose as starkly as possible the differences between history and myth, scholarship and error. These preoccupations were given a special impetus for many of us by the mounting interest in the Holocaust, which, we feared, might well decisively undermine attempts to write the history of East European Jews with sobriety and balance.

There was, and remains, much wisdom in this view. But it would be an error to overlook the ways in which extraacademic influences have inspired Russian Jewish history in the recent past, however indirectly. A frank acknowledgment of new influences outside the academy would not represent quite the break that some assume; similar influences have intruded (quite inevitably) on the writing of Russian Jewish history since its first appearance.

Moreover, the desire to redress the balance and mute the impact of folk memory might, in fact, have contributed to the exclusion of crucial aspects of the past from our historical purview. I wonder to what extent Jewish anxieties were overlooked in some of our historical work not only because of the difficulty of exploring these in the absence of archival data but also because of a rather excessive preoccupation with telling a different side of an all-too-familiar, grim narrative. For example, fear of military conscription among mid-nineteenth-century Russian Jewry is a theme that I'm now interested in. In the writing of my book on Odessa, prior to the opening of Russian archives, I did not have much material on the topic. However, I didn't think much about the problem, either. A willingness to confront seriously the anxieties of that community might make us more attuned to this, and similar, concerns.[12]

We find ourselves at an uncertain, intriguing crossroad in our knowledge of this region. Scholars from the West can anticipate the prospect of far greater intimacy with the region and an immeasurably deeper understanding of the terrain on which this history was conducted, leading to the production of new, archivally based scholarship where previously we had to rely primarily on printed sources accessible in Western libraries: pamphlets, newspapers, and books. Archives will now, almost certainly, allow a fuller appreciation of this community's everyday life, its vicissitudes as well as its pleasures. Such trips can also be put to good use in inspiring a familiarity with terrain, climate, food, and architecture of the sort that we so admire, say, in the historian of France Eugen Weber, whose intimacy with place, with fleeting, seemingly insignificant gestures and mannerisms, opens up a breadth of historical implications because of his receptivity to what he sees before him in the present.[13]

In contrast, so much of our own work has been written as if the very ground of the world we have captured historically was now blank, its remaining Jews silent: the term "the Jews of silence" that Elie Wiesel used and popularized was especially influential in the way it flattened and objectified Soviet Jews, in fact a garrulous, complex community. This, reinforced by the unavailability of archival material and obstacles to travel, lent a sometimes eerily abstract, distant texture to much of what we wrote.[14]

These issues seem especially pertinent to me now. As a historian of Russian Jewry, I have come to find it burdensome, and also less than useful, to sequester the Shoah as decisively as I had before in my work. This has been true for me since travel restrictions to Russia and Ukraine were lifted. Seeing Russia, Ukraine, and Poland has made me increasingly aware that as I think about the region, the catastrophe that obliterated so much of its Jewish world intrudes on my work. However much has changed in the region since World War II, it should come as little surprise that what we, from the West, are likely to see most powerfully are the killing fields of the recent past: the terrible chasm between the vibrant, vivid, flourishing world of pre-Nazi Jewish life and war's aftermath.

The insistence on dispassion that has figured so prominently in Russian Jewish historical writing since its beginnings was not quite so vexing before due to the physical distance separating most of us from it. The archival restrictions imposed as a result of Communist fiat shielded us from confronting with any immediacy what had transpired on that ground during World War II. Ironically, it was less cumbersome to imagine historically nineteenth-century Odessa or Berdichev before we were permitted to travel to the region than it is now. Seeing them as blank and empty served to protect us from thinking about the horrors that had overtaken them in the war. We did not need to wrestle with freeing ourselves from the horrors that the Soviet Jewish writer Vassily Grossman would later attach to the same place-names beginning in the mid-1940s: "There are no Jews in Ukraine. Nowhere—Poltava, Kharkov, Kremenchug . . . —in none of the cities, hundreds of the towns, or thousands of the villages will you see the black, tear-filled eyes of little girls; you will not hear the sad voice of an old woman; you will not see the dark face of a hungry baby. All is silence. Everything is still. A whole people have been brutally murdered." [15]

I had long before read these lines in Grossman's "Ukraine without Jews," but like other work that I had encountered about the catastrophe that befell Jews under Nazi rule, it had no impact, as I saw it, on how I wrote about the Ukraine. This remained true until for the first time I found myself, in the spring of 1993, on a train traversing its stunning, verdant, Jewishly resonant and also Jewishly empty countryside. The shock was enormous and it remains with me still.

Should we resist it when this new intimacy or, at least, knowledge of the terrain about which we write inspires an intense sense that these are the sites of East European Jewry's greatest horrors? When and if this occurs, should this sense be treated as little more than a distraction from serious work, as something to be excised? And would not such self-conscious omission make itself felt, too?

The following statements, both of which seek to weigh how the Holocaust might inform one's sense of the more distant past, have proven helpful to me in thinking about these problems. The first is a reflection on the wages of Jewish memory; the second is a dictum on the writing of Jewish history. I quote first from Saul Friedlander's brilliant memoir, *When Memory Comes*:

> We Jews erect walls around our most harrowing memories, and our most anxious thoughts of the future. Even a story complete to the last detail sometimes turns into an exercise in hiding things from ourselves. These necessary defenses are one of the chief features of our most profound dread. [16]

On the Holocaust

The second citation I draw from a new history of the Jews of Germany, the first volume in what promises to be an exemplary series of four books tracing German Jews from early modern times through the Holocaust. The books are to be edited by Michael Meyer and Michael Brenner. In the preface to the first volume, Meyer writes about the deliberations of his editorial board regarding the project:

> On certain issues we readily agreed. Despite the overwhelming reality of the Holocaust, which brought the history we relate here to a tragic close, we were intent on not viewing that history through its lens. We did not want hindsight to prejudice our analysis of earlier hopes. Yet we also decided not to minimize the role that antisemitism has played throughout the history of Jewish life in German lands. We had to recognize that a leitmotif of our narrative would be the trajectory from emancipation to exclusion and destruction.[17]

The price paid for the barriers that Jews (or, for that matter, others) erect between our worst experiences and our sense of the world is at the heart of Friedlander's observation. On the other hand, the role served by the same barriers as an essential strategy for a balanced, contextualized view of the present or past is at the crux of Michael Meyer's statement. It is difficult to disagree with either. It is important to note, however, that both challenge in rather different ways arguments already familiar to us. A forceful, recent reformulation of such arguments can be found in Michael Bernstein's book *Foregone Conclusions: Against Apocalyptic History*. According to this literary scholar, even a minimal preoccupation with the Holocaust when writing about the pre-Shoah Jewish past instills in the historian a harrowing, unlikely prescience that undermines the prospect of writing intelligently about the contingencies and contradictory possibilities so crucial to good history. He admires, as he tells us, the austere, perhaps (he admits) impossible goal set by Michael Ignatieff, who, when reviewing a few years ago books on the Jews of the Austro-Hungarian empire, stated: "In no field of historical study does one wish more fervently that historians could write history blind to the future." [18]

This is not what the more subtle Michael Meyer claims in his preface as either possible or, for that matter, desirable. Trajectory, he appreciates, is not the same as teleology. Still, although this is a fair distinction, it is by no means self-evident where the one begins and the other ends. In other words, although there is a distance separating Meyer's statement from Bernstein's warning regarding the long shadow cast by the Holocaust, if Meyer sees this past as beginning with emancipation and ending with destruction, how can the Holocaust not appear at the edge of his lens? The editors' choice of what to highlight, what to minimize, and how to build their narrative will, no doubt, be influenced by the reality of German Jewry's destruction. How is this different, then, from what Bernstein warns us to avoid as historically invalid and manipulative? And if the Holocaust intrudes in such ways on the text—as Meyer acknowledges that it must—why not evaluate these narrative choices openly in the books themselves if they are likely to weigh on their authors?

One must not overlook how readily the Holocaust can exert, as George Steiner has observed, a "corrupting fascination." It is this dangerous allure that Michael Bernstein criticizes most vigorously. Bernstein treats with particular disdain Ernst Pawel's well-known, widely praised biography of Franz Kafka, published in 1984. He cites Pawel's references to the Holocaust (an event that, of course, had no impact on Kafka's lamentably short life) as "shamelessly manipulative," in a book that is, he says, "dense with . . . embarrassing moments" such as "the description of Kafka's bar mitzvah: 'under Jewish law, Amschel, alias Franz Kafka, became a man on the morning of June 13, 1896 at the . . . Gypsy Synagogue, so called because of its location on a street formerly known as [Gypsy Street], though the strange name contains a chilling hint of things to come: a few decades later, the gypsies were to share the fate of the Jews.'"[19] This, Bernstein calls, rather grandly, a descent into "Hitler-kitsch,"[20] part of a whole network of contradictions in writings on the Shoah which he finds also in the fiction of Israeli writer Aron Appelfeld and others. As Bernstein writes, "I think that it is actually the critics themselves who, encountering Kafka in the aftermath of the Shoah, have become prophets-after-the-fact and have found themselves unable to read stories like "The Penal Colony" without thinking of the concentration camps."[21]

Frankly, why not? Perhaps to speak of the location of Kafka's synagogue as a "chilling hint" is a useless diversion, but my rereading of Pawel's biography finds it a vivid, original account of the man (if, perhaps, a less successful rendering of his art) which examines, as it must, Kafka's tragic sense of good and evil and the disproportionate sense of shame that, as Kafka taught us, overwhelms the relatively blameless but never quite guiltless and that is both terrible and hilarious. (Kafka, we're told, laughed heartily as he read drafts of "Metamorphosis" to his friends; indeed, the Kafka who emerges from Pawel's biography is a good deal more robust than in other biographical accounts.) In any event, how could the Holocaust not intrude on this narrative? I say this not because both *The Trial* and *The Castle* were saved, and just barely, from the Nazis and likely oblivion. More important, it is the discrete, mechanical horrors of rationality and bureaucracy that are, quite justly, the central concerns of

On the Holocaust

Pawel's book on Kafka, and although Pawel nowhere claims that Kafka foresaw Auschwitz (he makes it clear that he does not think this), he affirms the sentiments expressed in the obituary of Kafka written by his beloved, Milena Jesenska (in 1924). She writes of him that he was "condemned to see with such blinding clarity that he found [the world] unbearable."[22]

Two decades later, Prague's Jews were obliterated, Kafka's sisters were murdered, and Milena, too, was killed—and Bernstein expects the Berlin-born Ernst Pawel to write a biography of Kafka without a semblance of foreshadowing? Had these references to the Shoah (which don't intrude, it seems to me, on his masterful description of Kafka's life) been excised, their absence itself would likely have been apparent. This would have constituted an unnecessary subversion of the text in the name of self-restraint and dispassion, in the name of a silence without historical value, especially since the ravages of the Holocaust were clearly on Pawel's subtle, richly imaginative, brooding mind.

Peter Homans reminds us in his intriguing book *The Ability to Mourn* how psychoanalysis recognized that with the secularization of modern society came the loss of crucial sacred space for consolation.[23] Our new, all-too-fresh encounters with that "hole in the heart of the world" (as a new, popular study of Jewish life in contemporary Eastern Europe is entitled) can, I suspect, be integrated usefully into our work in reconstructing the Jewish past. An interesting experiment in this vein is a recent book by English-born documentary filmmaker Theo Richmond entitled *Konin: A Quest*. It is inspired, as he admits, by a preoccupation with the Holocaust, which destroyed his father's town in northwestern Poland. With almost deadpan, relentless meticulousness (along with the requisite self-awareness about what it is that moves him most as an author), he writes as full and vivid a portrait of a Polish Jewish community in the first decades of the twentieth century as we have in the English language. The motivation throughout is commemoration; the impetus is the Holocaust; the result is a very good history that would not have been quite as impressive, I'm convinced, had Richmond been less explicit about his goals and less self-aware about their execution in the text.[24]

Without really knowing that he is doing this, Richmond ignores many of the central rules set down (or, at least, taken for granted) by Jewish historians as to how to write effectively about the past. Yet the book succeeds admirably. Richmond acknowledges, for instance, his genealogical interests (although he, too, distrusts these impulses), and he unabashedly sees the book as an exercise in commemoration for a community devastated in World War II. It is written expressly to mark the passing of that community, especially to set down for posterity the names and the lore of his kin. It is this, he acknowledges, that motivated him to expend so much energy, time, and expense gathering whatever shards that remain of that history in England, the United States, Israel, and Konin itself. His preoccupation with the Holocaust does not, however, flatten his narrative; it prompts him to re-create with particular care and devotion Konin's streets, marketplaces, shops, schools, even its outhouses (itself the subject of a vivid, valuable chapter). Indeed, no East European Jewish historian has, to the best of my knowledge, in recent memory devoted a full chapter of a local history to lavatories or outhouses—further indication, perhaps, of the relatively rarefied nature of our own work in comparison with Richmond's, with its fixation on every last, accessible detail.

So, contrary to what one might otherwise expect of such

a book, Richmond's interest in the community's commemoration does not obscure for him the complex texture of everyday life. In fact, it helps make him all the more attentive to the people's routines, all the more skeptical of abstractions that might separate us from them, and all the more sensitive to the need to set down as full a record as possible. Richmond, a documentary filmmaker by training, has an especially good eye for detail, which, no doubt, assists him in this impressive, moving book. But the book also demonstrates something more fundamental: how a commemorative impulse can be harnessed effectively to expand one's sense of the past in ways that broaden its emotional, as well as intellectual, range.

"[N]o book, no work of art, can commemorate an exterminated culture. The existence of art presupposes the continuity of life; it cannot replace the life that was taken from us. Art must recognize this fact, for it is this that gives it its greatness: the simple recognition that life is greater." [25] So said the American Jewish literary critic Isaac Rosenfeld, that rare American-born Jewish writer who wrote a supple Yiddish as well as a splendid native English. He wrote these words in 1949. A few years earlier, in what had been a scholarly meeting of the YIVO Institute for Jewish Research, the young, Warsaw-born theologian Abraham Joshua Heschel delivered a stunning secular eulogy for the Jews of Eastern Europe (now known, in rather different form, as *The Earth Is the Lord's*) before a mostly Yiddishist, secular crowd who stood up at its end and spontaneously recited the Kaddish. [26] I better understand such reactions now. I better understand that they aren't quite so irrelevant to what I do as a historian. There is a special power to historical narratives that reveal, or at least appreciate clearly, from where they come—even when they start, or end, as laments. Recall the acute self-awareness of Irving Howe's lengthy, six-hundred-page lament for the Lower East Side and, above all, the world of his own father: "A story encompasses us, justifies our stay, prepares our leaving. Here, in these pages, is the story of the Jews, bedraggled and inspired, who came from eastern Europe. Let us now praise obscure men." [27] These are its last words. This is a book that started, and ended, as an evocation of one man's father. Howe in his wisdom understood well what the book was, and it was this acute, admirable self-understanding that helped inspire him to make it so much more.

"Writing what you know has nothing to do with security: What is more dangerous?" asks Eudora Welty. [28] I gain sustenance from those in the past whose achievements and biases, whose relationship to community and work, help me contextualize my own. Like them, I, too, sit scribbling, writing about what I love most and about what is most unsettling, which, if you're doing what you should, amounts to the same thing.

Notes

Prologue

1. Pierre Nora, "Between Memory and History: Les Lieux de Mé-moire, *Representations* 26 (spring 1989): 10.

2. I take the term "surplus of memory" from the English-language title of the autobiography of Warsaw ghetto fighter Yitzhak Zuck-erman, *A Surplus of Memory* (Berkeley and Los Angeles, 1993). For examples of recent work on how to write about Russian and East European Jewry, see Benjamin Harshav, *The Meaning of Yiddish* (Berke-ley and Los Angeles, 1990); Jack Kugelmass, "The Rites of the Tribe: The Meaning of Poland for American Jewish Tourists," *YIVO Annual* 21 (1993): 395–453; David Roskies, *A Bridge of Longing: The Lost Art of Yiddish Storytelling* (Cambridge, Mass., 1995); Ezra Mendelsohn, *On Modern Jewish Politics* (New York, 1993); Alain Finkelkraut, *The Imaginary Jew*, trans. Kevin O'Neill and David Suchoff (Lincoln, Nebr., 1994); Michael C. Steinlauf, *Bondage to the Dead: Poland and the Memory of the Holocaust* (Syracuse, 1997); Yael Zerubavel, *Recovered Roots: Collective Memory and the Making of Israeli National Tradition* (Chicago, 1995); Simon Schama, *Landscape and Memory* (New York, 1995), pp. 23–36; Jonathan Boyarin, *Thinking in Jewish* (Chicago, 1996).

3. See Arthur Hertzberg, *The Jews in America, Four Centuries of an Uneasy Encounter: A History* (New York, 1989), esp. pp. 152–76.

4. Alfred Kazin, introduction to *The Commentary Reader*, ed. N. Pod-horetz (New York, 1966), p. xx.

5. Quoted in Amos Funkenstein, *Perceptions of Jewish History* (Berkeley and Los Angeles, 1993), p. 8. See Maurice Halbwachs, *On Collective Memory*, trans. L. A. Coser (Chicago, 1992). Also see Eric Hobs-bawm, "Introduction: Inventing Traditions," in *The Invention of Tradi-*

tion, ed. E. Hobsbawm and T. Ranger (Cambridge, 1983), pp. 1–14; Steven Englund, "The Ghost of the Nation Past," *Journal of Modern History* 64 (June 1992): 299–320.

6. Funkenstein, *Perceptions of Jewish History*, p. 11.

7. Ibid., p. 19.

8. "Place in Fiction," in *The Eye of the Story: Selected Essays and Reviews*, by Eudora Welty (New York, 1990), pp. 129–30.

9. Eli Lederhendler, "Did Russian Jewry Exist Prior to 1917?" in *Jews and Jewish Life in Russia and the Soviet Union*, ed. Yaacov Ro'i (Illford, Essex, 1995), pp. 15–27.

10. David Lowenthal, *The Past Is a Foreign Country* (Cambridge, 1985); David Lowenthal, *Possessed by the Past: The Heritage Crusade and the Spoils of History* (New York, 1996); Saul Friedlander, *Memory, History, and the Extermination of the Jews of Europe* (Bloomington, 1993). Yosef Hayim Yerushalmi's brooding, intriguing *Zakhor: Jewish History and Jewish Memory* (Seattle, 1982) remains the most sustained examination of the relationship in Jewish life between history and memory.

11. Sylvia Teplinsky, *Collected Poems and Writings* (privately printed in Los Angeles, 1951).

1. Shtetls There and Here

For the quotation at the beginning of my chapter, I use the modified translation in Richard Terdiman, *Present Past: Modernity and the Memory Crisis* (Ithaca, 1993), p. 42.

1. Isaac Rosenfeld, *Passage from Home* (New York, 1946), p. 3.

2. Lionel Trilling, "Introduction," in *Collected Stories*, by I. Babel (New York, 1961), p. 21: "he thought about large and serious things, among them, respectability and fame. He was a shopkeeper, not well to do, a serious man, a failure. The sons of such men have much to prove, much to test themselves for, and, if they are Jewish, their Jewishness is ineluctably involved in the test." For a more accurate appraisal of Babel's (actually rather well-to-do) family background, based on information readily available only since the late 1980s, see Carol J. Avins's introduction to Isaac Babel's *1920 Diary*, trans. H. T. Willets (New Haven,

1990), pp. xvii–lviii. On Trilling's own family background, see Diana Trilling, *The Beginning of the Journey* (New York, 1993).

3. Rosenfeld, *Passage from Home*, p. 11.

4. Isaac Rosenfeld, "The Situation of the Jewish Writer," in *Preserving the Hunger: An Isaac Rosenfeld Reader*, ed. Mark Shechner (Detroit, 1988), pp. 122–23. The essay appeared originally in *Contemporary Jewish Record* 7, no. 1 (1944). On Rosenfeld, see Theodore Solataroff's introduction to his collection of Rosenfeld's essays, *An Age of Enormity* (Cleveland, 1962), pp. 15–40, and Mark Shechner's introduction to *Preserving the Hunger*, pp. 21–37. More generally, see Steven J. Zipperstein, "Commentary and American Jewish Culture in the 1940s and '50s," *Jewish Social Studies: History, Culture, and Society* 3, no. 2 (winter 1997): 18–28. An indication of the impact of *Passage from Home* on writers at the time was its inspiration of lengthy ruminations by both Irving Howe (a rare, revealing autobiographical essay) and Daniel Bell. See Irving Howe, "The Lost Intellectual: A Marginal Man, Twice Alienated," *Commentary*, Oct. 1949, pp. 361–67; and Daniel Bell, "A Parable of Alienation," reprinted in the *Jewish Frontier Anthology, 1945–1967* (New York, 1967), pp. 41–62.

5. Shechner, *Preserving the Hunger*, p. 267. This story was published shortly after Rosenfeld's death in July 1956. It appeared in *Midstream* 2, no. 1 (1956). I've discovered in private hands a handwritten copy of a (slightly different) Yiddish-language version.

6. Werner Sollors, "Literature and Ethnicity," in *Harvard Encyclopedia of American Ethnic Groups*, ed. S. Thernstrom, A. Orlov, and O. Handlin (Cambridge, Mass., 1980), p. 663.

7. Jack Kugelmass, "Green Bagels: An Essay on Food, Nostalgia, and the Carnivalesque," *YIVO Annual* 19 (1990): 73–74; David Margolick, "Jewish Comics Make It a Not So Silent Night," *New York Times*, 24 Dec. 1994, p. 23.

8. For an indication of the vast body of source material available for such studies of popular culture, see *National Jewish Archive of Broadcasting: Catalogue of Holdings* (New York, 1995); and Jenna Weissman Joselit, *The Wonders of America: Reinventing Jewish Culture, 1880–1950* (New York, 1994).

9. On Kaplan's Lithuanian childhood, see Mel Scult, *Judaism Faces*

Notes to Chapter 1

the Twentieth Century: A Biography of Mordecai M. Kaplan (Detroit, 1993), pp. 19–28. I thank Eli Lederhendler for suggesting to me the connection between Kaplan's use of the term "organic community" and an abiding, albeit muted preoccupation with East European Jewry.

10. Quoted in Ronald Sanders, *The Downtown Jews* (New York, 1969), pp. 429–30.

11. Several recent studies have examined this theme in various ways: Ewa Morawska, "Changing Images of the Old Country in the Development of Ethnic Identity among East European Immigrants, 1880–1930s: A Comparison of Jewish and Slavic Representations," *YIVO Annual* 21 (1993): 272–73; Ewa Morawska, *Insecure Prosperity: Small Town Jews in Industrial America, 1890–1940* (Princeton, 1996), pp. 3–71; Eli Lederhendler, *Jewish Responses to Modernity: New Voices in America and Eastern Europe* (New York, 1994), pp. 104–39; Matthew Frye Jacobson, *Special Sorrows: The Diasporic Imaginations of Irish, Polish, and Jewish Immigrants in the United States* (Cambridge, Mass., 1995), pp. 54–93.

12. Morawska, "Changing Images of the Old Country," p. 286.

13. Mary Antin, *The Promised Land* (Cambridge, Mass., 1912), p. 1.

14. Ibid.

15. In the 1960 edition of Cahan's *The Rise of David Levinsky*, Levinsky proclaims, "I discover America," on p. 83.

16. Ibid., p. 91.

17. See Isaac Rosenfeld, "David Levinsky: The Jew as American Millionaire," in *An Age of Enormity*, pp. 273–81.

18. Cahan, *Rise of David Levinsky*, p. 61.

19. See Moses Rischin's excellent introduction to Hutchins Hapgood, *The Spirit of the Ghetto* (Cambridge, Mass., 1967), pp. vii–xxxvi.

20. Rischin contrasts Hapgood's account with Riis's in ibid., pp. xxiii–xxiv.

21. Hapgood, *Spirit of the Ghetto*, p. 11. I refer here, of course, to Irving Howe, *World of Our Fathers: The Journey of the East European Jews to America and the Life They Found and Made* (New York, 1976).

22. The cover of the 1959 Meridian paperback edition of Maurice Samuel's *The Prince of the Ghetto* (New York, 1948) promises a "revelation of the life and world of Polish Jewry through a retelling of the tales of the Yiddish master, Isaac Loeb Peretz."

23. Deborah Dash Moore, *At Home in America: Second Generation New York Jews* (New York, 1981), p. 9.

24. Irving Howe, "The New York Intellectuals," in *Selected Writings, 1950–1990* (New York, 1990), p. 241.

25. Alfred Kazin, *A Walker in the City* (New York, 1951), p. 61.

26. Howe, "Strangers," in *Selected Writings*, p. 330.

27. For a perceptive interpretive essay on Yezierska, see Mary V. Dearborn, "Anzia Yezierska and the Making of an Ethnic American Self," in *The Invention of Ethnicity*, ed. Werner Sollors (New York, 1989), pp. 105–23.

28. Anzia Yezierska, *Bread Givers* (New York, 1925), p. 33.

29. Ibid., p. 208.

30. Anzia Yezierska, *Red Ribbon on a White Horse* (New York, 1950), p. 77.

31. Kazin, introduction to *The Commentary Reader*, ed. Norman Podhoretz (New York, 1966), p. xx.

32. Delmore Schwartz, "The World Is a Wedding," in *"In Dreams Begin Responsibilities" and Other Stories* (New York, 1978), p. 38.

33. Ibid., pp. 38–39.

34. Delmore Schwartz, "A Bitter Farce," in *The World Is a Wedding* (Norfork, Conn., 1948), p. 103.

35. Deborah E. Lipstadt, "America and the Memory of the Holocaust, 1950–1965," *Modern Judaism* 16 (1996): 197. Also see Alvin H. Rosenfeld, "The Americanization of the Holocaust," *Commentary* 99 (June 1995).

36. For a discussion of the use to which Anne Frank was put in American culture, as seen through the lens of Meyer Levin's intense and abiding preoccupation with the play based on Anne Frank's diary, see Lawrence Garven, *An Obsession with Anne Frank* (Berkeley and Los Angeles, 1995).

37. Howe, "The New York Intellectuals," in *Selected Writings*, pp. 264–65.

38. Norman Podhoretz, "Jewish Culture and Intellectuals: The Process of Rediscovery," *Commentary*, May 1955, pp. 451–56. Also see Midge Decter, "Belittling Sholom Aleichem's Jews: Folk Falsification of the Ghetto," *Commentary*, May 1954, pp. 389–92.

39. For a discussion of the background to the writing of *Life Is with*

People, whose author, Mark Zborowski, was an admitted—indeed, particularly successful—Communist agent, see Barbara Kirshenblatt-Gimblett's new introduction to *Life Is with People: The Culture of Shtetl Life* (New York, 1995), pp. ix–xlviii. Also see my essay "The Shtetl Revisited," in *Shtetl Life: The Nathan and Faye Hurvitz Collection* (Berkeley, 1993), pp. 17–24.

40. Janet Hadda, *Isaac Bashevis Singer: A Life* (New York, 1997), pp. 131, 164.

41. Ibid., p. 164.

42. Ibid.

43. The story (translated from Yiddish by Isaac Rosenfeld) is included in Irving Howe and Eliezer Greenberg, *A Treasury of Yiddish Stories* (New York, 1954), pp. 523–43.

44. "Landmark Symposium: *Fiddler on the Roof*, Peter Stone, Moderator, Jerry Brock, Sheldon Harnick, Joseph Stein," *Dramatists' Guild Quarterly* 20 (spring 1983): 14. Also see the excellent article by Seth Wolitz, "The Americanization of Tevye or Boarding the Jewish Mayflower," *American Quarterly* 40 (Dec. 1988): 514–36. For the text of *Fiddler on the Roof*, see Joseph Stein, *Fiddler on the Roof* (New York, 1968). Also see Ken Frieden, "A Century of Sholem Aleichem's 'Tevye,'" in *The B. G. Rudolph Lectures in Jewish Studies, New Series* (Syracuse, N.Y., 1997).

45. Irving Howe, "Tevye on Broadway," *Commentary*, Nov. 1964, p. 74.

46. Richard Altman, with Mervyn Kaufman, *The Making of a Musical: Fiddler on the Roof* (New York, 1971), p. 31; "Landmark Symposium," p. 12.

47. "Landmark Symposium," p. 14.

48. Altman, *Making of a Musical*, p. 39.

49. Ibid., p. 31.

50. Ibid., p. 18.

51. See Wolitz's analysis, "The Americanization of Tevye," p. 529.

52. Maurice Samuel, *The World of Sholom Aleichem* (New York, 1947).

53. Scott Donaldson, *The Suburban Myth* (New York, 1969), pp. 18–19, 59, 118, 122; William H. Whyte, *The Organization Man* (New York,

1956); Robert C. Wood, *Suburbia: Its People and Their Politics* (Boston, 1959); Richard Yates, *Revolutionary Road* (Boston, 1961), p. 237.

54. Seymour Leventman, "From Shtetl to Suburb," in *The Ghetto and Beyond: Essays on Jewish Life in America*, ed. Peter Rose (New York, 1969), p. 52. On Jews in suburbia in the 1950s and early 1960s, see Arthur A. Goren, "A 'Golden Decade' for American Jews: 1945–1955," *Studies in Contemporary Jewry* 8 (1992): 3–20; Albert I. Gordon, *Jews in Suburbia* (Boston, 1959); Herbert Gans, "Progress of a Suburban Jewish Community," *Commentary* 21 (1957): 113–22; Judith R. Kramer, *Children of the Gilded Ghetto: Conflict Resolution of Three Generations of American Jews* (New Haven, 1961); Samuel C. Heilman, *Portrait of American Jews: The Last Half of the 20th Century* (Seattle, 1995), pp. 19–32.

55. Sol Gittleman, *From Shtetl to Suburbia* (Boston, 1978), p. 148.

56. Philip Roth, "Eli, the Fanatic," in *Goodbye, Columbus* (Boston, 1959), p. 215.

57. Ibid., p. 181.

58. Ibid., p. 191.

59. Ibid., p. 189.

60. Ibid., p. 216.

2. Reinventing Heders

1. Chaim Weizmann, *Trial and Error* (New York, 1949), p. 4.

2. Cahan, *Rise of David Levinsky*, p. 21.

3. The quotation from Isaac Ber Levinsohn can be found in Dov Baer (Bernard) Natanson, *Sefer ha-zikhronot, divrei yemei Rihal* (Warsaw, 1889), p. 13. Shimon Dubnow's article (signed S.D.) is entitled "Mstislavl' (Mogilevsk. gub.)." It appeared in *Russkii evrei*, no. 37 (12 Sept. 1880): cols. 1455–56. See also S. J. Abramowitz, "Mah anu?" *Ha-Shahar* 6 (1875); Shmuel Werses, "Jewish Education in 19th Century Russia in the Eyes of Mendele Mocher Seforim," in *Jewish Education and Learning*, ed. Glenda Abramson and Tudor Parfitt (Chur, Switzerland, 1994), pp. 243–60; Steven J. Zipperstein, "Transforming the Heder: Maskilic Politics in Imperial Russia," in *Jewish History: Essays in Honour of Chimen Abramsky*, ed. Ada Rapoport-Albert and Steven J.

Notes to Chapter 2

Zipperstein (London, 1988), pp. 87–109; and Shaul Stampfer, "Heder Study, Knowledge of Torah, and the Maintenance of Social Stratification in Traditional East European Jewish Society," in *Studies in Jewish Education*, vol. 3 (Jerusalem, 1988), pp. 271–89. The most comprehensive study of heders in the Russian empire remains *Sovremennyi kheder* (St. Petersburg, 1912).

4. Eliezer Meir Lipshutz, *Ketavim*, vol. 1 (Jerusalem, 1947), p. 319.

5. See the summary by journalist M. Levin in *Voskhod*, no. 14 (1903): 10–13.

6. Dr. L. L. Rokhlin, "K voprosu o sanitarnom sostoianii khederov v g. Kharkove," *Evreiskii meditsinskii golos* 1, nos. 2–3 (1 July 1908). This is a detailed document, 28 pages in length, with charts and bibliography.

7. *Sovremennyi kheder*, pp. 8, 14, 18, 31–32.

8. Ibid., p. 42.

9. Ibid., p. 3.

10. Dan Miron, "Folklore and Antifolklore in the Yiddish Fiction of the Haskalah," in *Studies in Jewish Folklore*, ed. Frank Talmage (Cambridge, Mass., 1980), p. 233.

11. G. Vol'tke, "Kheder i melamed (v Rossii i Tsarstve Pol'skom)," in *Evreiskaia entsiklopediia* (St. Petersburg, [1906–13]), vol. 15, cols. 590–96.

12. *Voskhod*, no. 4 (1903): 4, 7.

13. There is much literature on the *heder metukan*. Kh[ayyim] A[ryeh] Zuta, *Bereshit darki* (Jerusalem, 1934), is the fullest memoiristic account of the movement. Yitzhak Epstein, "Irvit be-ivrit," *Ha-Shiloach* (Nov. 1898): 385–96, was credited with having helped inspire it.

14. Kh[ayyim] Zuta, *Ha-melamed ve-ha-moreh* (Jerusalem, [1913 or 1914]), p. 5.

15. Zuta, *Bereshit darki*, p. 145.

16. Ibid., p. 146.

17. Zuta refers to this transcript in *Bereshit darki*, p. 146. The title of the transcript, in Special Collections, National and University Library, Jerusalem, is in Zuta's hand: "Din ve-heshbon shel asefat ha-morim ha-ivrim be-Orsha (ve'idat ha-morim ha-ivrim ha-rishonim)."

18. For the comments by Ilion and Lifshits see "Asefat," pp. 6, 7.

19. "Asefat," pp. 3, 4, 7, 8. Comparisons with schools elsewhere, most often in England, were typical in these pedagogical circles. See the discussion of English public schools as a prototype for Jewish education in *Protokol komiteta dlia rasprostraneniia prosveshcheniia mezhdu evreiami v Rossii, 24–27 dekabria 1902 g.* (St. Petersburg, 1903), p. 64.

20. *Voskhod*, nos. 51–52 (1904): 39–41.

21. *Voskhod*, no. 45 (1903): 19.

22. Zuta, *Bereshit darki*, p. 146.

23. Hans Rogger, *Russia in the Age of Modernisation and Revolution, 1881–1917* (London, 1983), pp. 182–83.

24. Jeffrey Brooks, *When Russia Learned to Read: Literacy and Popular Literature, 1861–1917* (Princeton, 1985), p. 218.

25. See M. Rafes, *Ocherki po istorii "Bunda"* (Moscow, 1923). For a definitive history of the Bund's ideological transformation in imperial Russia, see Jonathan Frankel, *Prophecy and Politics: Socialism, Nationalism, and the Russian Jews, 1862–1917* (Cambridge, 1981), pp. 171–257.

26. *K voprosu o natsional'nom vospitanii* (Odessa, 1903); Steven J. Zipperstein, *Elusive Prophet: Ahad Ha'am and the Origins of Zionism* (Berkeley and Los Angeles, 1993), pp. 183–87.

27. *Voskhod*, no. 45 (1903): 20–21.

28. *Ensiklopediah hinukhit*, vol. 4 (Jerusalem, 1964), pp. 579–82, 590–91.

29. *Ha-Shiloach* 17 (1907): 417–22.

30. Ibid., pp. 420, 422.

31. *Evreiskaia shkola*, no. 1 (1904): 3–9.

32. "Asefat," p. 8.

33. Shimon Dubnow, *Kniga zhizni*, vol. 1 (Riga, 1934), p. 176.

3. Remapping Odessa

1. I[osif] V[ladimirovich] Gessen, *V dvukh vekakh: zhizenennyi otchet* (Berlin, 1937), pp. 10–11.

2. Ibid., pp. 12–14, 17–18.

3. Ibid., p. 13.

4. Ibid., p. 19.

Notes to Chapter 3

5. See *Odessa, 1794–1894: Izdanie gorodskogo obshchestvennogo upravleniia k stoletiiu goroda* (Odessa, 1895), p. 145; Steven J. Zipperstein, *The Jews of Odessa: A Cultural History, 1794–1881* (Stanford, 1985), pp. 20–21.

6. Zipperstein, *Jews of Odessa*, pp. 47– 49, 131–33.

7. A. M. Gudvan, *Ocherki po istorii dvizheniia sluzhashchikh v Rossii* (Moscow, 1925). See the excerpts in Victoria E. Bonnell, ed., *The Russian Worker: Life and Labor under the Tsarist Regime* (Berkeley and Los Angeles, 1983). I thank Victoria E. Bonnell for providing me with a copy of this rare book. I cite here Isaac Babel, *Collected Stories*, trans. David McDuff (London, 1994), p. 253.

8. Cecile Kuznitz, "On the Jewish Street: Yiddish Culture and the Urban Landscape in Interwar Vilna," in *Yiddish Language and Culture, Then and Now: Proceedings of the Ninth Annual Klutznick Symposium* (Omaha, 1999).

9. Shmuel Feiner, *Me-haskalah lohemet le-haskalah meshameret* (Jerusalem, 1993); Arcadius Kahan, "Vilna: The Sociocultural Anatomy of a Jewish Community in Interwar Poland," in *Essays in Jewish Social and Economic History* (Chicago, 1986), pp. 149– 60; David G. Roskies, *Against the Apocalypse: Responses to Catastrophe in Modern Jewish Culture* (Cambridge, Mass., 1984), pp. 1–14 and passim.

10. Stuart Hampshire, "Commitment and Imagination," in *The Morality of Scholarship*, ed. Max Black (Ithaca, 1962), p. 46; also see Edward Said, *Beginnings: Intention and Method* (New York, 1975), pp. 12–13.

11. See Steven J. Zipperstein, "Russian Maskilim and the City," in *The Legacy of Jewish Migration: 1881 and Its Impact*, ed. David Berger (New York, 1983), pp. 31– 45.

12. Dubnow, *Kniga zhizni*, vol. 1, p. 246.

13. *Kitvei E[lhonon] L. Levinsky*, vol. 2 (Tel Aviv, 1913), pp. 495–97.

14. Ibid., pp. 497–98.

15. Quoted in Naomi Seidman, *A Marriage Made in Heaven: The Sexual Politics of Hebrew and Yiddish* (Berkeley and Los Angeles, 1997), p. 40.

16. Y[itshak] D[ov] Berkowitz, *Ha-rishonim ki-vene adam* (Tel Aviv, 1975–76), p. 1003.

17. Yosef Klausner, *Historiya shel ha-sifrut ha-ivrit ha-hadasha*, vol. 5 (Jerusalem, 1955), p. 364. A valuable, detailed discussion of this novel

Notes to Chapter 4

may be found in David Patterson, *The Hebrew Novel in Czarist Russia* (Edinburgh, 1964).

18. Reuven Braudes, *Shete ha-ketsavot* (Jerusalem, 1989), p. 40.

19. Ibid., p. 89.

20. Ibid., p. 53.

21. Ibid., p. 60.

22. Yaakov Fichman, *Sofrim be-heyehem* (Tel Aviv, 1942), pp. 5–6.

23. There is a large body of memoirs produced by such intellectuals. An incisive analysis of this literature may be found in Dan Miron, *Bodedim bemoadam* (Tel Aviv, 1987), pp. 23–111. Also see Marcus Moseley, "Jewish Autobiography in Eastern Europe: The Prehistory of a Literary Genre" (D.Phil., Trinity College, Oxford, 1990). Moseley's superb work is slated for publication by Stanford University Press.

24. See the description of this circle in Zipperstein, *Elusive Prophet*, esp. pp. 67–72.

25. The passage, published originally in the 1888 Hebrew journal *Kaveret*, is reprinted in *Kol kitvei Ahad Ha'am* (Jerusalem, 1956), p. 115; I translated it originally for *Elusive Prophet*, pp. 18–19.

26. Quoted in Lowenthal, *The Past Is a Foreign Country*, p. 52. Sontag's article, "Unguided Tour," appeared in the *New Yorker*, 31 Oct. 1977.

27. Babel, "How It Was Done in Odessa," in *Collected Stories*, pp. 184–85.

4. On the Holocaust

1. This chapter was first presented in February 1997 as the keynote address of the UCLA Center for European Studies conference "East Central European Jewish Communities since the Holocaust." I dedicated it to my Russian history mentor, Hans Rogger, as an expression of my gratitude to him as a teacher and friend.

2. David Lowenthal, "Nostalgia Tells It Like It Wasn't," in *The Imagined Past: History and Nostalgia*, ed. Christopher Shaw and Malcolm Chase (Manchester, 1989). For an example of the value of such insights in the examination of Jewish historical consciousness, see Jack Kugelmass, "The Rites of the Tribe: The Meaning of Poland for American Jewish Tourists," *YIVO Annual* 21 (1993): 395–453.

3. Shimon Dubnow, *Ob izuchenii istorii evreev* (St. Petersburg,

1891); Shimon Dubnow, "Nahpesah venahkorah," *Pardes* (Odessa) 1 (1892): 221–41. The article was issued the same year as a separate pamphlet. I quote from the original piece in *Pardes*. For assessments of Dubnow's achievements as a historian, see Jonathan Frankel, "S. M. Dubnov: Historian and Ideologue," in Sophie Dubnov-Erlich, *The Life and Work of S. M. Dubnov* (Bloomington, 1991), pp. 1–33; Robert M. Seltzer, "Simon Dubnow: A Critical Biography of His Early Years" (Ph.D. diss., Columbia University, 1970); David H. Weinberg, *Between Tradition and Modernity* (New York, 1996). Dubnow described his decision to produce the Hebrew-language version of *Ob izuchenii*, in his *Kniga zhizni*, vol. 1, p. 269. For an interesting attempt to test Dubnow's contemporary relevance for historians of Russian Jewry, see Eli Lederhendler, "The Politics of Cultural Transmission, the Legacy of Simon Dubnov, and Jewish Studies," in his *Jewish Responses to Modernity*, pp. 189–97.

4. Dubnow, "Nahpesah," p. 226.

5. "If only our ancestors had left us a *Shulchan Aruch* for history," Dubnow laments ("Nahpesah," p. 225). The diary entry is cited in Dubnow, *Kniga zhizni*, vol. 1, p. 268.

6. Dubnow, *Kniga zhizni*, vol. 1, pp. 269–70.

7. On Russian and East European Jewish historiography, see Gershon David Hundert and Gershon C. Bacon, *The Jews in Poland and Russia: Bibliographical Essays* (Bloomington, 1984); Avraham Greenbaum, "The Beginnings of Jewish Historiography in Russia," *Jewish History* 7, no. 1 (spring 1993): 99–105; Shmuel Feiner, *Haskalah vehistoriah* (Jerusalem, 1995); Ezra Mendelsohn, "Interwar Poland: Good or Bad for the Jews?" in *The Jews in Poland*, ed. Chimen Abramsky, Maciej Jachimczyk, and Antony Polonsky (Oxford, 1986), pp. 130–39. More specifically, see the article by Marcus Moseley, "Between Memory and Forgetfulness: The Janus Face of Michah Yosef Berdichevsky," *Studies in Contemporary Jewry* 12 (1996): 78–117.

8. Steven J. Zipperstein, "Old Ghosts: Pogroms in the Jewish Mind," *Tikkun* 6, no. 3 (May/June 1991).

9. Alfred Greenbaum, *Jewish Scholarship and Scholarly Institutions in Soviet Russia, 1918–1953* (Jerusalem, 1977).

10. Schama, *Landscape and Memory*, pp. 27–28.

11. See Philip Roth, *Reading Myself, and Others* (New York, 1985).

12. The preponderance of cantonist narratives, written by Jews conscripted as youth into the Russian army under Tsar Nicholas I (1825–55), published, often in annotated form, in the first journals devoted to the Russian Jewish past (*Evreiskaia starina* and *Perezhitoe*) is, for example, a topic that merits further examination. Such work might help us better understand the preoccupations of Jews in late imperial Russia. Cantonist narratives were recorded then in these journals no doubt partly because their authors were nearing death; they also, arguably, were a relatively safe, muted way of speaking about the rigors of contemporary tsarist life.

13. Mark von Hagen, "The Archival Gold Rush and Historical Agendas in the Post-Soviet Era," *Slavic Review* 52, no. 1 (spring 1993): 96–100. A good indication of the vast, still on the whole unexplored archival material on Jewish themes in the former Soviet Union may be found in Dorit Sallis and Marek Web, eds., *Jewish Documentary Sources in Russia, Ukraine, and Belarus: A Preliminary List* (New York, 1996). Eugen Weber is best known for *Peasants into Frenchmen* (Stanford, 1976).

14. For an examination of Wiesel's influence on contemporary readings of the East European Jewish past, see Naomi Seidman, "Elie Wiesel and the Scandal of Jewish Rage," *Jewish Social Studies: History, Culture, and Society* 3, no. 1 (fall 1996): 1–19.

15. Quoted in John Gerrard and Carol Gerrard, *The Bones of Berdichev: The Life and Fate of Vasily Grossman* (New York, 1996), p. 170.

16. Saul Friedlander, *When Memory Comes* (New York, 1979), p. 75.

17. Michael Meyer, ed., *German Jewish History in Modern Times*, vol. 1 (New York, 1996), p. x.

18. Michael Andre Bernstein, *Foregone Conclusions: Against Apocalyptic History* (Berkeley and Los Angeles, 1996), p. 16.

19. Bernstein, *Foregone Conclusions*, p. 18. The passage criticized by Bernstein is in Ernst Pawel, *The Nightmare of Reason: A Life of Franz Kafka* (New York, 1984), p. 60.

20. Bernstein, *Foregone Conclusions*, p. 18.

21. Ibid., p. 21.

22. Mary Hockaday, *Kafka, Love and Courage: The Life of Milena Jesenska* (Woodstock, N.Y., 1997), p. 113.

23. Peter Homans, *The Ability to Mourn: Disillusionment and Social Origins of Psychoanalysis* (Chicago, 1989); Jonathan Kaufman, *A Hole in the Heart of the World: Being Jewish in Eastern Europe* (New York, 1997); Dominick LaCapra, *Representing the Holocaust: History, Theory, Trauma* (Ithaca, 1994), pp. 215–17.

24. Theo Richmond, *Konin: A Quest* (New York, 1995). Richmond's book is written in the vein of *yizker bikher*, the memorial books produced (mostly in Israel) by survivors and descendants of East European Jewish communities. On the use of this literature as history, see Jack Kugelmass and Jonathan Boyarin, eds. and trans., *From a Ruined Garden: The Memorial Books of Polish Jewry* (New York, 1983).

25. Isaac Rosenfeld, "Images of a Lost World," in *Preserving the Hunger*, ed. Mark Shechner, p. 145.

26. The original version of Heschel's text can be found in *Der mizrekh-eyropeisher yid* (New York, 1946). For an illuminating discussion of Heschel as a writer, see Jeffrey Shandler, "Heschel and Yiddish: A Struggle with Signification," *Journal of Jewish Thought and Philosophy* 2, no. 2 (1993): 245–300.

27. Howe, *World of Our Fathers*, p. 646.

28. Welty, "Place in Fiction," in her *Eye of the Story*, p. 130.

Bibliography

Books

Abramsky, Chimen, Maciej Jachimczyk, and Antony Polansky, eds. *The Jews in Poland*. Oxford: B. Blackwell, 1986.

Altman, Richard, with Mervyn Kaufman. *The Making of a Musical: Fiddler on the Roof*. New York: Crown Publishers, 1971.

Antin, Mary. *The Promised Land*. Cambridge, Mass.: Houghton Mifflin, 1912.

Babel, Isaac. *1920 Diary*. Trans. H. T. Willets. New Haven: Yale University Press, 1990.

Berger, David, ed. *The Legacy of Jewish Migration: 1881 and Its Impact*. New York: Brooklyn College Press; distributed by Columbia University Press, 1983.

Berkowitz, Y[itshak] D[ov]. *Ha-rishonim ki-vene adam*. Tel Aviv: Devir, 1975–76.

Bernstein, Michael Andre. *Foregone Conclusions: Against Apocalyptic History*. Berkeley and Los Angeles: University of California Press, 1996.

Black, Max, ed. *The Morality of Scholarship*. Ithaca: Cornell University Press, 1962.

Bonnell, Victoria E., ed. *The Russian Worker: Life and Labor under the Tsarist Regime*. Berkeley and Los Angeles: University of California Press, 1983.

Boyarin, Jonathan. *Thinking in Jewish*. Chicago: University of Chicago Press, 1996.

Braudes, Reuven. *Shete ha-ketsavot*. Jerusalem: Mosad Byalik, 1989.

Brooks, Jeffrey. *When Russia Learned to Read: Literacy and Popular Literature, 1861–1917*. Princeton: Princeton University Press, 1985.

Bibliography

Cahan, Abraham. *The Rise of David Levinsky*. New York: Harper, 1960.

Donaldson, Scott. *The Suburban Myth*. New York: Columbia University Press, 1969.

Dubnov-Erlich, Sophie. *The Life and Work of S. M. Dubnov*. Trans. Judith Vowles. Bloomington: Indiana University Press, 1991.

Dubnow, Shimon. *Kniga zhizni*. Vol. 1. Riga, 1934.

———. *Ob izuchenii istorii evreev*. St. Petersburg, 1891.

Ensiklopediah hinukhit. Vol. 4. Jerusalem, 1964.

Feiner, Shmuel. *Me-haskalah lohemet le-haskalah meshameret*. Jerusalem: Merkaz Dinur, 1993.

———. *Haskalah ve-historiah*. Jerusalem: Merkaz Zalman Shazar le-toldot Yisrael, 1995.

Fichman, Yaakov. *Sofrim be-heyehem*. Tel Aviv: Masadah, 1942.

Fin, Samuel Joseph. *Kiryah ne'emanah*. Vilna: Romm, 1860.

Finkelkraut, Alain. *The Imaginary Jew*. Trans. Kevin O'Neill and David Suchoff. Lincoln, Nebr.: University of Nebraska Press, 1994.

Frankel, Jonathan. *Prophecy and Politics: Socialism, Nationalism, and the Russian Jews, 1862–1917*. Cambridge: Cambridge University Press, 1981.

Friedlander, Saul. *Memory, History, and the Extermination of the Jews in Europe*. Bloomington: Indiana University Press, 1993.

———. *When Memory Comes*. New York: Farrar, Straus, Giroux, 1979.

Funkenstein, Amos. *Perceptions of Jewish History*. Berkeley and Los Angeles: University of California Press, 1993.

Garrard, John, and Carol Garrard. *The Bones of Berdichev: The Life and Fate of Vasily Grossman*. New York: Free Press, 1996.

Garvin, Lawrence. *An Obsession with Anne Frank*. Berkeley and Los Angeles: University of California Press, 1995.

Gessen, I[osif] V[ladimirovich]. *V dvukh vekakh: zhizenennyi, otchet*. Berlin: Speer und Schmidt, 1937.

Gittleman, Sol. *From Shtetl to Suburbia*. Boston: Beacon Press, 1978.

Gordon, Albert I. *Jews in Suburbia*. Boston: Beacon Press, 1959.

Greenbaum, Alfred. *Jewish Scholarship and Scholarly Institutions in Soviet Russia, 1918–1953*. Jerusalem: Hebrew University of Jerusalem, Centre for Research and Documentation of East European Jewry, 1977.

Bibliography

Gudvan, A. M. *Ocherki po istorii dvizheniia sluzhashchikh v Rossii.* Moscow: TSK SSTS, 1925.

Hadda, Janet. *Isaac Bashevis Singer: A Life.* New York: Oxford University Press, 1997.

Hapgood, Hutchins. *The Spirit of the Ghetto.* Cambridge, Mass.: Belknap Press of Harvard University Press, 1967.

Halbwachs, Maurice. *On Collective Memory.* Trans. Lewis A. Coser. Chicago: University of Chicago Press, 1992.

Harshav, Benjamin. *The Meaning of Yiddish.* Berkeley and Los Angeles: University of California Press, 1990.

Heilman, Samuel C. *Portrait of American Jews: The Last Half of the 20th Century.* Seattle: University of Washington Press, 1995.

Hertzberg, Arthur. *The Jews in America, Four Centuries of an Uneasy Encounter: A History.* New York: Simon and Schuster, 1989.

Hobsbawm, Eric, and Terence Ranger, eds. *The Invention of Tradition.* Cambridge: Cambridge University Press, 1983.

Hockaday, Mary. *Kafka, Love and Courage: The Life of Milena Jesenska.* Woodstock, N.Y.: Overlook Press, 1997.

Homans, Peter. *The Ability to Mourn: Disillusionment and Social Origins of Psychoanalysis.* Chicago: University of Chicago Press, 1989.

Howe, Irving. *Selected Writings, 1950–1990.* New York: Harcourt Brace Jovanovich, 1990.

———. *World of Our Fathers: The Journey of the East European Jews to America and the Life They Found and Made.* New York: Harcourt Brace Jovanovich, 1976.

Howe, Irving, and Eliezer Greenberg, eds. *A Treasury of Yiddish Stories.* New York: Viking Press, 1954.

Hundert, Gershon David, and Gershon C. Bacon. *The Jews in Poland and Russia: Bibliographic Essays.* Bloomington: Indiana University Press, 1984.

Jacobson, Matthew Frye. *Special Sorrows: The Diasporic Imaginations of Irish, Polish, and Jewish Immigrants in the United States.* Cambridge, Mass.: Harvard University Press, 1995.

Joselit, Jenna Weissman. *The Wonders of America: Reinventing Jewish Culture, 1880–1950.* New York: Hill and Wang, 1994.

K voprosu o natsional'nom vospitanii. Odessa, 1903.

Bibliography

Kaufman, Jonathan. *A Hole in the Heart of the World: Being Jewish in Eastern Europe*. New York: Viking, 1997.

Kazin, Alfred. *A Walker in the City*. New York: Harcourt, Brace, 1951.

Klausner, Yosef. *Historiya shel ha-sifrut ha-ivrit ha-hadasha*. Vol. 5. Jerusalem, 1955.

Kol kitvei Ahad Ha'am. Jerusalem, 1956.

Kramer, Judith R. *Children of the Gilded Ghetto: Conflict Resolution of Three Generations of American Jews*. New Haven: Yale University Press, 1961.

Kugelmass, Jack, and Jonathan Boyarin, eds. and trans. *From a Ruined Garden: The Memorial Books of Polish Jewry*. New York: Schocken Books, 1983.

LaCapra, Dominick. *Representing the Holocaust: History, Theory, Trauma*. Ithaca: Cornell University Press, 1994.

Lederhendler, Eli. *Jewish Responses to Modernity: New Voices in America and Eastern Europe*. New York: New York University Press, 1994.

Lipschutz, Eliezer Meir. *Ketavim*. Vol. 1. Jerusalem: Mosad ha-Rav Kuk, 1947.

Lowenthal, David. *The Past Is a Foreign Country*. Cambridge: Cambridge University Press, 1985.

———. *Possessed by the Past: The Heritage Crusade and the Spoils of History*. New York: Free Press, 1996.

Mendelsohn, Ezra. *On Modern Jewish Politics*. New York: Oxford University Press, 1993.

Meyer, Michael, ed. *German Jewish History in Modern Times*. Vol. 1. New York: Columbia University Press, 1996.

Miron, Dan. *Bodedim bemoadam*. Tel Aviv: Am Oved, 1987.

Moore, Deborah Dash. *At Home in America: Second Generation New York Jews*. New York: Columbia University Press, 1981.

Morawska, Ewa. *Insecure Prosperity: Small Town Jews in Industrial America, 1890–1940*. Princeton: Princeton University Press, 1996.

Moseley, Marcus. "Jewish Autobiography in Eastern Europe: The Prehistory of a Literary Genre." D.Phil. diss., Trinity College, Oxford, 1990.

Natanson, Dov Baer (Bernard). *Sefer ha-zikhronot, divrei yemei Ribal*. Warsaw: B. Natansona, 1889.

Bibliography

National Jewish Archive of Broadcasting: Catalogue of Holdings. New York: The Jewish Museum, 1995.

Odessa, 1794–1894: Izdanie gorodskogro obshchestvennogo upravleniia k stoletiiu goroda. Odessa: A. Shul'tse, 1895.

Patterson, David. *The Hebrew Novel in Czarist Russia*. Edinburgh: University Press, 1964.

Pawel, Ernst. *The Nightmare of Reason: A Life of Franz Kafka*. New York: Farrar, Straus, Giroux, 1984.

Podhoretz, Norman, ed. *The Commentary Reader*. New York: Atheneum, 1966.

Protokol komiteta dlia rasprostraneniia prosveshcheniia mezhdu evreiami v Rossii, 24–27 dekabria 1902 g. St. Petersburg, 1903.

Rafes, M. *Ocherki po istorii "Bunda."* Moscow: Moskovskii Rabochii, 1923.

Richmond, Theo. *Konin: A Quest*. New York: Pantheon Books, 1995.

Rogger, Hans. *Russia in the Age of Modernisation and Revolution, 1881–1917*. London: Longman, 1983.

Rose, Peter, ed. *The Ghetto and Beyond: Essays on Jewish Life in America*. New York: Random House, 1969.

Rosenfeld, Isaac. *Passage from Home*. New York: Dial Press, 1946.

Roskies, David G. *Against the Apocalypse: Responses to Catastrophe in Modern Jewish Culture*. Cambridge, Mass.: Harvard University Press, 1984.

———. *A Bridge of Longing: The Lost Art of Yiddish Storytelling*. Cambridge, Mass.: Harvard University Press, 1995.

Roth, Philip. *Goodbye, Columbus*. Boston: Houghton Mifflin, 1959.

———. *Reading Myself, and Others*. New and expanded ed. New York: Penguin, 1985.

Ryden, Kent C. *Mapping the Invisible Landscape*. Iowa City: University of Iowa Press, 1993.

Said, Edward. *Beginnings: Intention and Method*. New York: Basic Books, 1975.

Sallis, Dorit, and Marek Web, eds. *Jewish Documentary Sources in Russia, Ukraine, and Belarus: A Preliminary List*. New York: Jewish Theological Seminary of America, 1996.

Samuel, Maurice. *The Prince of the Ghetto*. New York: A. A. Knopf, 1948.

Bibliography

————. *The World of Sholom Aleichem*. New York: Knopf, 1947.

Sanders, Ronald. *The Downtown Jews*. New York: Harper and Row, 1969.

Schama, Simon. *Landscape and Memory*. New York: A. A. Knopf, 1995.

Schwartz, Delmore. *"In Dreams Begin Responsibilities" and Other Stories*. New York: New Directions, 1978.

————. *The World Is a Wedding*. Norfolk, Conn.: New Directions, 1948.

Scult, Mel. *Judaism Faces the Twentieth Century: A Biography of Mordecai M. Kaplan*. Detroit: Wayne State University Press, 1993.

Seidman, Naomi. *A Marriage Made in Heaven: The Sexual Politics of Hebrew and Yiddish*. Berkeley and Los Angeles: University of California Press, 1997.

Seltzer, Robert M. "Simon Dubnow: A Critical Biography of His Early Years." Ph.D. diss., Columbia University, 1970.

Shaw, Christopher, and Malcolm Chase, eds. *The Imagined Past: History and Nostalgia*. Manchester: Manchester University Press, 1989.

Shechner, Mark, ed. *Preserving the Hunger: An Isaac Rosenfeld Reader*. Detroit: Wayne State University Press, 1988.

Solataroff, Theodore, ed. *An Age of Enormity*. Cleveland: World Publishing, 1962.

Sovremennyi kheder. St. Petersburg, 1912.

Stein, Joseph. *Fiddler on the Roof*. New York: Pocket Books, 1968.

Steinlauf, Michael C. *Bondage to the Dead: Poland and the Memory of the Holocaust*. Syracuse, N.Y.: Syracuse University Press, 1997.

Talmage, Frank, ed. *Studies in Jewish Folklore*. Cambridge, Mass.: Association for Jewish Studies, 1980.

Teplinsky, Sylvia. *Collected Poems and Writings*. Privately printed in Los Angeles, 1951.

Terdiman, Richard. *Present Past: Modernity and the Memory Crisis*. Ithaca: Cornell University Press, 1993.

Tonnies, Ferdinand. *Community and Society*. Trans. Charles P. Loomis. New York: Harper and Row, 1963.

Trilling, Diana. *The Beginning of the Journey*. New York: Harcourt Brace, 1993.

Weber, Eugen. *Peasants into Frenchmen*. Stanford: Stanford University Press, 1976.

Bibliography

Weinberg, David H. *Between Tradition and Modernity*. New York: Holmes and Meier, 1996.

Weizmann, Chaim. *Trial and Error*. New York: Harper, 1949.

Welty, Eudora. *The Eve of the Story: Selected Essays and Reviews*. New York: Random House, 1978. Reprint, 1990.

Whyte, William Hollingsworth. *The Organization Man*. New York: Simon and Schuster, 1956.

Wood, Robert C. *Suburbia: Its People and Their Politics*. Boston: Houghton Mifflin, 1959.

Yates, Richard. *Revolutionary Road*. Boston: Little Brown, 1961.

Yerushalmi, Yosef Hayim. *Zakhor: Jewish History and Jewish Memory*. Seattle: University of Washington Press, 1982.

Yezierska, Anzia. *Bread Givers*. New York: Doubleday, Page, 1925.

———. *Red Ribbon on a White Horse*. New York: Scribner, 1950.

Zborowski, Mark. *Life Is with People: The Culture of Shtetl Life*. New York: Schocken, 1995.

Zerubavel, Yael. *Recovered Roots: Collective Memory and the Making of Israeli National Tradition*. Chicago: University of Chicago Press, 1995.

Zipperstein, Steven J. *Elusive Prophet: Ahad Ha'am and the Origins of Zionism*. Berkeley and Los Angeles: University of California Press, 1993.

———. *The Jews of Odessa: A Cultural History, 1794–1881*. Stanford, Calif.: Stanford University Press, 1985.

Zuckerman, Yitzhak. *A Surplus of Memory*. Berkeley and Los Angeles: University of California Press, 1993.

Zuta, Kh[ayyim] A[ryeh]. *Bereshit darki*. Jerusalem, 1934.

———. *Ha-melamed ve-ha-moreh*. Jerusalem: Defus Ahdut, [1913 or 1914].

Articles

Abramowitz, S. J. "Mah anu?" *Ha-Shuhar* 6 (1875).

Bell, Daniel. "A Parable of Alienation." In *Jewish Frontier Anthology, 1945–1967*. New York: Jewish Frontier Association, 1967.

Dearborn, Mary V. "Anzia Yezierska and the Making of an Ethnic

Bibliography

American Self." In *The Invention of Ethnicity*, ed. Werner Sollors. New York: Oxford University Press, 1989.

Decter, Midge. "Belittling Sholom Aleichem's Jews: Folk Falsification of the Ghetto." *Commentary*, May 1954.

Dubnow, Shimon. "Mstislavl' (Mogilevsk. gub.)." *Russkii evrei* 37 (12 Sept. 1880).

———. "Nahpesah venahkorah." *Pardes* (Odessa) 1 (1892).

Englund, Steven. "The Ghost of the Nation Past." *Journal of Modern History* 64 (June 1992).

Epstein, Yitzhak. "Irvit be-ivrit." *Ha-Shiloach* (Nov. 1898).

Frieden, Ken. "A Century of Sholem Aleichem's 'Tevye.'" In *The B. G. Rudolph Lectures in Jewish Studies, New Series*. Syracuse, N.Y.: Syracuse University Press, 1997.

Gans, Herbert. "Progress of a Suburban Jewish Community." *Commentary* 21 (1957).

Goren, Arthur A. "A 'Golden Decade' for American Jews: 1945–1955." *Studies in Contemporary Jewry* 8 (1992).

Greenbaum, Avraham. "The Beginnings of Jewish Historiography in Russia." *Jewish History* 7, no. 1 (spring 1993).

Howe, Irving. "The Lost Intellectual: A Marginal Man, Twice Alienated." *Commentary*, Oct. 1949.

———. "Tevye on Broadway." *Commentary*, Nov. 1964.

Kahan, Arcadius. "Vilna: The Sociocultural Anatomy of a Jewish Community in Interwar Poland." In *Essays in Jewish Social and Economic History*. Chicago: University of Chicago Press, 1986.

Kugelmass, Jack. "Green Bagels: An Essay on Food, Nostalgia, and the Carnivalesque." *YIVO Annual* 19 (1990).

———. "The Rites of the Tribe: The Meaning of Poland for American Jewish Tourists." *YIVO Annual* 21 (1993).

Kuznitz, Cecile. "On the Jewish Street: Yiddish Culture and the Urban Landscape in Interwar Vilna." In *Yiddish Language and Culture, Then and Now: Proceedings of the Ninth Annual Klutznick Symposium*. Omaha: University of Nebraska Press, 1999.

"Landmark Symposium: *Fiddler on the Roof*, Peter Stone, Moderator, Jerry Brock, Sheldon Harnick, Joseph Stein." *Dramatists' Guild Quarterly* 20 (spring 1983).

Bibliography

Lederhendler, Eli. "'Did Russian Jewry Exist Prior to 1917?" In *Jews and Jewish Life in Russia and the Soviet Union*, ed. Yaacov Ro'i. Illford, Essex: F. Cass, 1995.

Lipstadt, Deborah E. "America and the Memory of the Holocaust, 1950–1965." *Modern Judaism* 16 (1996).

Margolick, David. "Jewish Comics Make It a Not So Silent Night." *New York Times*, 24 Dec. 1994, p. 23.

Martone, Michael. "Correctionville, Iowa." *North American Review*, Dec. 1991.

Morawska, Ewa. "Changing Images of the Old Country in the Development of Ethnic Identity among East European Immigrants, 1880–1930s: A Comparison of Jewish and Slavic Representations." *YIVO Annual* 21 (1993).

Moseley, Marcus. "Between Memory and Forgetfulness: The Janus Face of Michah Yosef Berdichevsky." *Studies in Contemporary Jewry* 12 (1996).

Nora, Pierre. "Between Memory and History: Les Lieux de Mémoire." *Representations* 26 (spring 1989).

Podhoretz, Norman. "Jewish Culture and Intellectuals: The Process of Rediscovery." *Commentary*, May 1955.

Rokhlin, L. L. "K voprosu o sanitarnom sostoianii khederov v g. Kharkove." *Evreiskii meditsinskii golos* 1, nos. 2–3 (1 July 1908).

Rosenfeld, Alvin H. "The Americanization of the Holocaust." *Commentary* 99 (June 1995).

Rosenfeld, Isaac. "The Situation of the Jewish Writer." *Contemporary Jewish Record* 7, no. 1 (1944).

Seidman, Naomi. "Elie Wiesel and the Scandal of Jewish Rage." *Jewish Social Studies: History, Culture, and Society* 3, no. 1 (fall 1996).

Shandler, Jeffrey. "Heschel and Yiddish: A Struggle with Signification." *Journal of Jewish Thought and Philosophy* 2, no. 2 (1993).

Sollors, Werner. "Literature and Ethnicity." In *Harvard Encyclopedia of American Ethnic Groups*, ed. Stephen Thernstrom, Ann Orlov, and Oscar Handlin. Cambridge, Mass.: Belknap Press of Harvard University, 1980.

Stampfer, Shaul. "Heder Study, Knowledge of Torah, and the Maintenance of Social Stratification in Traditional East European

Bibliography

Jewish Society." In *Studies in Jewish Education*, vol. 3. Jerusalem: Magnes Press, 1988.

Vol'tke, G. "Kheder i melamed (v Rossii i Tsarstve Pol'skom)." In *Evreiskaia entsiklopediia*, vol. 15. St. Petersburg: Izdanie Obshchestva dlia Nauchnykh Evreiskikh Izdanii i Izdatelstva Brokhaus-Efron, [1906–13].

von Hagen, Mark. "The Archival Gold Rush and Historical Agendas in the Post-Soviet Era." *Slavic Review* 52, no. 1 (spring 1993).

Werses, Shmuel. "Jewish Education in 19th Century Russia in the Eyes of Mendele Mocher Seforim." In *Jewish Education and Learning*, ed. Glenda Abramson and Tudor Parfitt. Chur, Switzerland: Harwood Academic Publishers, 1994.

Wolitz, Seth. "The Americanization of Tevye, or Boarding the Jewish Mayflower." *American Quarterly* 40 (Dec. 1988).

Zipperstein, Steven J. "Commentary and American Jewish Culture in the 1940s and '50s." *Jewish Social Studies: History, Culture, and Society* 3, no. 2 (winter 1997).

———. "Old Ghosts: Pogroms in the Jewish Mind." *Tikkun* 6, no. 3 (May/June 1991).

———. "The Shtetl Revisited." In *Shtetl Life: The Nathan and Faye Hurvitz Collection*. Berkeley: Judah L. Magnes Museum, 1993.

———. "Transforming the Heder: Maskilic Politics in Imperial Russia." In *Jewish History: Essays in Honour of Chimen Abramsky*, ed. Ada Rapoport-Albert and Steven J. Zipperstein. London: Halban, 1988.

Index

Index

Index

Index

29–30; impact of past Russian Jewish images on, 9; in suburbs, 37–38. *See also* community

ideologies: of Odessa intellectuals, 83; and popular attitudes, 4; in Russian historiography, 93. *See also* nationalism

Ignatieff, Michael, 100

Ilion, B. S., 52, 57

immigration: American laws, 24; from "Darkest Russia," 93; intellectual interest in, 30–31; materialistic immigrant, 23; as point of reference, 24–25, 27–28; and surplus of memory, 4

In Bluebeard's Castle (Steiner), 41

intellectuals in Odessa, 77–85; marginality of, 79–80, 83–84

Jabotinsky, Vladimir, 64, 70

"Jerusalem of Lithuania," 67

Jesenska, Milena, 102

Jewish press, 20, 21, 49, 69

Jewish Socialist Labor Bund, 53–54, 56

Jews without Money (Gold), 18

journals: of Odessa intellectuals, 82, 84; as sources, 69–70. *See also* newspapers; press

Judaism, religious, heders and, 53

Kafka, Franz, 100–102

Kaplan, Mordecai, 19, 110*n*9

Kaveret, 82, 84

Kazin, Alfred, 5, 25, 28

"Ketavim balim" (A tattered manuscript) (Ahad Ha'am), 84–85

Kharkov: heders in, 44; Jewish enrollment quotas in schools of, 58

Kiryah ne'emanah (Fin), 68

Klausner, Joseph, 73

Konin: A Quest (Richmond), 102–4, 120*n*24

Kugelmass, Jack, 18

Kulbak, Moshe, 68

Lahishin, 12–13

Landscape and Memory (Schama), 94

language: "national values" and teaching of, 52–53; Rosenfeld and, 25, 104; Russian census classification determined by, 55. *See also* Hebrew language; Russian language; writing; Yiddish language

Levin, Meyer, 111*n*36

Levinsky, Elhonon, 71–72, 83

Levinsohn, Isaac Ber, 42

libraries, lending, 59, 60

Life Is with People (Zborowski), 31, 111–12*n*39

Lifshits, Gershon, 52, 54–55, 57

Lilienblum, Moshe Leib, 83

Lipshutz, Eliezer Meir, 43

Lipstadt, Deborah E., 29–30

literature: by American Jews, 16–18, 19, 21–39; Eastern Europe as chastisement in, 30; heder in, 42; on heders, 47–48; *yizker bikher*, 120*n*24; Holocaust and, 29–30, 32, 38, 100–102; shtetls in, 31, 32, 34–35; as sources of research, 96; on suburbia, 34–35, 36–39; *tref posul*, 80; on Vilna, 68. *See also* essays; fiction; journals; novels; reading; short stories; writing

134

Index

Lithuania: non-Jews from, 20. *See also* Vilna

"Little Shoemakers" (Singer), 32–33

liturgical exposition, and history, 7

London, Jewish elite in, 93

Los Angeles, intellectuals' view of, 70

Lowenthal, David, 11, 88

"Lo zeh ha-derekh" (This is not the way) (Ahad Ha'am), 84

Marek, Piotr, 59–60

Martone, Michael, 63

maskilim: and heders, 43; Odessa, 79–85. *See also* Enlightenment; intellectuals in Odessa

materialism: of immigrants, 23; of Odessa Jews, 64, 65–66, 70–71

"Matzoh Meal, MuShu, and Mistletoe" celebration, 18

McCarthyism, 12, 31

medical criticism of heders, 43–44

Melamed ve-ha-moreh, Ha- (The melamed and the teacher) (Zuta), 49–50

melameds: community and, 48; memories of, 42–43; new national teacher vs., 49–50; surveys of, 44–45. *See also* heders

Melting Pot (Zangwill), 18

memoirs: Friedlander, 98, 99; Kazin, 25; Odessa in, 70–72, 80–81, 83, 117*n23*. *See also* autobiography

memory: "collective," 6–7, 82, 95; "folk," 6–7; of heders/melameds, 42–43; history and, 3, 5–8, 11, 92–93, 95–96, 98, 99, 108*n10*; Odessa intellectuals and, 82; surplus of, 4, 107*n2*. *See also* nostalgia

Mendele Mocher Seforim, 42, 72–73, 81, 82–83

"Metamorphosis" (Kafka), 101

Meyer, Michael, 99, 100

military conscription of mid-nineteenth-century Russian Jewry, 96, 119*n12*; in Yezierska novel, 25

Miron, Dan, 45–46

modernity and Odessa, 80, 81. *See also* Enlightenment

Moore, Deborah Dash, 24

Morawska, Ewa, 20–21

Moseley, Marcus, 117*n23*

Mstislavl, 42–43, 60–62

narrative strategy, 11, 68, 100, 104–5

nationalism: and heders, 46–47, 49–58, 60; meaning of, 55–56; non-Zionist, 55–56. *See also* Ahad Ha'am; Zionism

Nazis, 94, 97, 98, 101. *See also* Holocaust

New Russia, heders in, 44–45

newspapers: Jewish, 21, 49, 69; lending-library readers of, 59; as sources, 69–70, 96. *See also* journals; press

1920 Diary (Babel), 87

Nora, Pierre, 3

nostalgia: Russia/Eastern Europe as object of, 4–5, 20, 29–30, 61–62. *See also* memory; sentimentality

Index

novels: by American Jews, 16–18, 19, 21–37; on Odessa, 70–71, 73–77; youth reading, 59

Odessa, 10, 63–86; Brodskaia Synagogue, 78; cultural institutions, 66, 70, 71–72; Gessen family, 64–65; *hakhmei Odessa* ("wise men of Odessa"), 81, 85; heders, 43–44; imagining vs. traveling in, 97; intellectuals, 77–82; "least historical of all cities," 70; materialism of Jews in, 64, 65–66; OPE branch, 54; school Jewish enrollment quotas, 58; State Archives, 78

OPE (Society for the Promotion of Enlightenment among Jews; Obshchestvo dlia rasprostraneniia prosvescheniia mezhdu evreiami v Rossii), 44–45, 48–57, 60

"organic community," Kaplan on, 19, 110*n*9

Organization Man (Whyte), 37

Ornitz, Samuel, 27

Orsha, teachers' meeting in, 50–53, 60

Pale of Settlement: lending libraries, 60; majority of Jews in, 9; schools, 44–45, 58

Passage from Home (Rosenfeld), 16–17, 109*n*4

patriarchy, in *Fiddler*, 36, 38

Pawel, Ernst, 100–102

"Penal Colony, The" (Kafka), 101

Peretz, Isaac Loeb, 31, 110*n*22

Plotsk, 21

Podhoretz, Norman, 30–31

poetry on Vilna, 68

pogroms, 4, 5, 93; in *Fiddler*, 33; Lahishin and, 12; teaching history of, 52; in Yezierska novel, 25–26

Poland: American Jews from, 21; heders, 44, 46; Konin commemoration, 102–4; non-Jews from, 20–21; Peretz tales and, 110*n*22; press in America, 21; Jewish historiography produced in, 93; travel to, 97; in Yezierska novels, 25–26

politics: and heders, 47, 53–54; left-wing, 13, 25, 48, 56, 112*n*39; Russian liberal party (Cadets), 64; Russian linguistic, 55. *See also* nationalism; Zionism

Poltava, library lending statistics from, 59

popular culture, 19; and ideologies, 4; representation of materialistic immigrant in, 23; Odessa, 78; responses in America to the Old World, 10, 15–39. *See also* fiction; popular memory; sentimentality

popular memory, historiography and, 3, 5–8, 11, 92–93, 95–96, 98, 99

population: Russian census, 55; Vilna and Odessa Jewish, 68

positivism, Dubnow's, 91

press: heder reform issue in, 49; Polish (in America), 21; Russian, 69; Yiddish (in America), 20, 21. *See also* journals; newspapers

Prince of the Ghetto, The (Samuel), 110*n*22

Promised Land (Antin), 21

psychoanalysis and mourning, 102

Index

reading: by Jewish youth, 59; by melameds, 44–45; *mevinim benomim* (middlebrow readers), 59; by Odessa Jews, 64–65, 71, 75, 84. *See also* libraries; literature; press

Red Ribbon on a White Horse (Yezierska), 26–28

Revolutionary Road (Yates), 37

Richmond, Theo, 102–4, 120*n24*

Riesman, David, 37

Riis, Jacob, 23

Rise of David Levinsky (Cahan), 22–23

ritual, Jewish, Gessen family, 65

Robbins, Jerome, 35

Rogger, Hans, 117*n1*

Rosenfeld, Isaac, 104; on Chekhov writing in Yiddish, 25; death, 109*n5*; *Passage from Home*, 16–17, 109*n4*; "World of the Ceiling," 17

Roth, Henry, 18

Roth, Philip, 19, 34–35, 38–39, 95

Rovno, heders in, 45

Russia/Eastern Europe: American Jewry imagining, 10, 15–39, 97; American non-Jews from, 20–21; archival availability, 69–70, 78, 79, 88–89, 91–92, 95–97; census, 55; "Darkest Russia," 93; ethnic heterogeneity, 9–10, 55–56; Lahishin and, 12–13; Mendele tour, 72–73; military conscription, 25, 96, 119*n12*; as object of nostalgia, 4–5, 20, 29–30, 61–62; Odessa Jews assimilating culture of, 65, 66; Odessa as main grain-exporting port, 66; Soviet, 4, 69, 82, 93–94;

suffering of Jews of, 93; travel to, 97, 98; tsarist, 4, 10, 26, 55–56, 93, 119*n12*; violence (1950s memories), 5; Zionism in, 4. *See also* heders; Odessa; Poland; Russian/Eastern European Jewish historiography; Russian Jewry; shtetls; Ukraine

Russian/Eastern European Jewish historiography, 5–6, 9, 10, 11, 68, 87–105; archival availability, 69–70, 78, 79, 88–89, 91–92, 95–97; Dubnow, 42–43, 70, 82, 89–92; first, 68; and Holocaust, 11, 87, 94, 95, 97–105; intellectuals central in, 77–79, 82; and popular memory, 3, 5–8, 11, 92–93, 95–96, 98, 99; sources, 68–71, 78–79, 88–89, 91–92, 95–97; Zionist, 4, 48

Russian Jewry: Americanization of, 20–21; anxiety about cultural erosion, 10, 45–62; current restricted knowledge of, 48; historical consciousness, 89–90; integrationist, 56, 57; most "modern" in Odessa, 80; strategies for maintaining culture, 60. *See also* immigration; memory; nationalism; Russia/Eastern Europe; Russian/Eastern European Jewish historiography

Russian language: American Jews and, 11–12; Dubnow's readers, 61; in heders, 55; Jewish newspapers in, 69; lending-library readers of, 59

Russianness, anxiety about, 55–56

Russian Orthodox Church, 55

Index

Index

This book is written for
my son & daughter, who
like I used to be - are
to pre-occupied with their own
wonderful & complicate lives
to be curious as to mine.
My father took with him to the
grave the answers to the
questions I did not ask.

I wish to set the record—
not so much straight, as for the
for their consideration & for you,
O stranger to my heart, mind, & soul—
may it lend you some light - & help
to make you yourself
and readier to take on this paradoxical more curious, more doubtful,
life with humor, courage & with love.